MEDITATIONS

DOVER THRIFT EDITIONS

Marcus Aurelius

DOVER PUBLICATIONS, INC.
MINEOLA, NEW YORK

DOVER THRIFT EDITIONS

GENERAL EDITOR: PAUL NEGRI
EDITOR OF THIS VOLUME: WILLIAM KAUFMAN

Copyright

Bibliographical Note

This Dover edition, first published in 1997, is a revised and updated version of George Long's translation of the *Meditations*, first published as *The Thoughts of the Emperor M. Aurelius Antoninus* by Bell of London in 1862. A new introduction has been specially prepared for this edition.

Library of Congress Cataloging-in-Publication Data

Marcus Aurelius, Emperor of Rome, 121–180.
   [Meditations. English]
   The meditations / by Marcus Aurelius ; the George Long translation, revised and updated.
      p.   cm. — (Dover thrift editions)
   ISBN-13: 978-0-486-29823-8
   ISBN-10: 0-486-29823-X
   1. Ethics. 2. Stoics. 3. Life. I. Long, George, 1800–1879. II. Title. III. Series.
B580.L6   1997
188—dc21   97-18832
                                                            CIP

Manufactured in the United States by LSC Communications
29823X25   2019
www.doverpublications.com

Table of Contents

Introduction

SEVERAL YEARS AGO *The New York Times Book Review* was obliged to create a splinter category, "Advice, How-to, and Miscellaneous," to ensure that traditional nonfiction books were not altogether bumped from its best-seller list. The titles in this booming "self-help" genre are often mere come-ons for the more costly emotional liniments peddled by the sages of the midnight infomercial: audiotapes, videotapes, seminars, retreats. Its spiritual void seemingly untouched by traditional religion and the blandishments of prosperity, the American middle class wanders the carnival tent of New Age healers and prophets, hell-bent on buying the happiness that money can't buy.

This is not a new story. A spiritual malaise also pervaded the unprecedented peace and wealth of the Roman Empire, driving its citizens away from their ethically sterile traditional paganism and into the arms of Eastern religions (or, to the Roman establishment, cults) such as Zoroastrianism, Mithraism, and Christianity. It was also a fertile atmosphere for Stoicism, an intellectually rigorous and ethically bracing Greek philosophy that thrived among the Roman nobility, eventually producing a masterpiece of ethical reflection in Marcus Aurelius's *Meditations*, which one commentator has called "one of the noblest products of the ancient mind." Far from promising snappy solutions and slick solace, however, the *Meditations* instructs and inspires through its calm and unblinking reckoning with the elemental difficulties of human life and its emphasis on virtue rather than pleasure as the key to inner peace.

Stoicism

Stoicism, having flowed through some five hundred years of Greek and Roman history, is not so much a single systematic doctrine as a winding intellectual current. Arising and flourishing amidst the uncertainties of the Hellenistic domain of the third century B.C.—a time of political and social upheaval following the deaths of Aristotle (322 B.C.) and Alexander the Great (323 B.C.)—Stoicism stressed the search for inner peace and ethical certainty despite the apparent chaos of the external world by emulating in one's personal conduct the underlying orderliness and lawfulness of nature.

Since the writings of the founding Stoics—Zeno of Citium (Cypress), Cleanthes of Assos, and Chrysippus of Soli—survive only in fragments, summaries of their ideas are perforce somewhat conjectural, based on citations in later writers. (The philosophy gets its name from the *stoa poikile* [painted colonnade] in Athens, where Zeno often held forth.) Several key elements of the early Stoics emerge clearly, however. Dividing philosophy into physics, logic, and ethics, they sought to unify theory and practice in a comprehensive cosmology. In contrast to Plato and Aristotle, for whom the highest realities were spiritual or ideational, the Stoics held that the essence of reality was material, arguing that an incorporeal soul could not direct the activities of a corporeal body. Unlike the purposeless, dead matter of modern variants of materialism, this elemental "stuff" of the universe is an ever-living creative fire, a divinity, in fact, that forms all life; physics and theology converge in a materialist pantheism. This living "stuff" has several names: God, Zeus, creative fire, ether, the word or reason (*logos*), order, law of destiny, fate. Through varying degrees of tension or tonicity, the primal fire spawns the various things of the world in cycles; in each *periodos* or *magnus annus* it gradually separates into four elements (water, earthly fire, air, and earth); eventually conflagration again reduces all to the elemental fire, which then expands into the universe once again, and so on for eternity, each cycle an exact repetition of the last.

While avowing the divine presence in all things, Zeno disdained the panoply of institutional religion, rejecting temples and rituals and stressing rather the worship of God through inner affirmation and outward virtue. The Stoic discovers the model for his virtuous conduct in studying the laws of nature; just as each object, plant, and animal serves its fated role in the larger order, so the human strives to steer his actions in accordance with his unique power, reason, his inner mirror of the *logos* that governs the universe. By focusing on those things that are within his power—his own will and perception—and detaching himself from the things that are not—health, death, the actions of others, natural disasters, and so on—he attains the inner peace (*eudaimonia*) of the wise and just man. This cultivated detachment (*apatheia*), achieved through disciplined self-restraint and moderation (*sophrosyne*), applies as well to the worldly allures of sensual indulgence, power, and fame, which the Stoic abjures not from puritanical repugnance but from his concern to free the soul for undistracted service to the *logos*.

Apatheia does not equal apathy, however. The *logos* of Stoicism is not a fate to be passively acknowledged but a spiritual potential to be actively won through intellectual and practical effort. Moreover, the universality of reason enjoins a social consciousness that embraces the just life not only for oneself but for all humanity under the "fatherhood of God" (*logos spermatikos*). In Marcus's words, "The prime principle in man's constitution is the social." Transcending the parochial confines of class, tribe, and nationality, the *logos* obliges each "citizen of the universe" to help in building what Maxwell Staniforth has aptly called a "cosmopolis that would be the very image of the rationally ordered physical world."

The social consciousness of Stoicism is not, however, a summons to the activism of mass movements. Civic virtue is a mirage unless anchored in the inner virtue of each citizen; for the Stoic the best antidote to outer turmoil is inner peace. In Marcus's words, "How much trouble he avoids who does not look to see what his neighbor says or does or thinks, but only to what he does himself, that it may be just and pure." And elsewhere he writes, "For nowhere either with more quiet or more freedom from trouble does a man retire than into his own soul, particularly when he has within him such thoughts that by looking into them he is immediately in perfect tranquillity." Thus does the Stoic define himself as a rational being in the face of all that beggars rationality. In Shakespeare's words, "There is nothing either good or bad, but thinking makes it so." Marcus, quoting the Cynic Monimus, puts it even more succinctly: "All is opinion."

Marcus Aurelius

The ethical precepts of Stoicism found a receptive audience among the practical, worldly citizens of ancient Rome. The chief early proponents of Stoic philosophy in Rome—Panaetius and Posidonius—dwelled on its ethical and religious teachings, convinced that Chrysippus's emphasis on theoretical physics robbed the tradition of its moral grandeur. Later in the Republic and early in the Empire, currents of Stoic thought ran through the writings of prominent thinkers such as Cicero, Cato, and Seneca. Epictetus, a former slave whose teachings influenced Marcus Aurelius, focused on nurturing one's *dai-*

mon (a much-used term in the *Meditations*), the divine spirit of reason and conscience in each human.

Marcus Aurelius Antoninus, one of the wisest and noblest of Roman emperors, was a direct heir to this rich tradition. He was born Marcus Annius Verus to a patrician family on April 26, A.D. 121. Both his parents having died young, he was adopted by his grandfather, under whose care he evidently passed a studious and happy childhood, schooled by a series of private tutors in the precepts of Stoicism, which he embraced wholeheartedly at the age of twenty-five, devoting himself to studies under Rusticus the Stoic.

Marcus's path to the throne was a circuitous one. Hadrian's first choice as his successor, Lucius Ceionius Commodus, died in 138, whereupon Hadrian adopted Titus Antoninus Pius (Marcus's uncle) with the understanding that Titus would adopt both Commodus's son and Marcus (whose full name then became Marcus Aelius Aurelius Antoninus), seemingly setting up a dual succession. Upon Hadrian's death that year, Marcus, at age seventeen, began, in effect, a twenty-three-year apprenticeship for the emperorship, serving in a variety of important governmental posts while continuing his philosophical studies. Before Titus died in 161, he recommended Marcus alone as his successor; Marcus magnanimously insisted that his adoptive brother, Lucius Verus, share the emperorship despite the latter's apparent lack of real ability or political support.

Marcus's reign was beset by natural disaster and war. An outbreak of plague spread panic throughout the western Empire; when vast stores of grain were spoiled by floods, Marcus sold his precious jewelry to help abate the resulting suffering; Quadi and Marcomanni tribesmen breached the borders of Pannonia, forcing Marcus to leave Rome for two years in order to take personal command of the threatened legions on the Danube, where he finally secured peace with the Marcomanni in 168. He was left sole emperor upon the death of Verus in 169; later an outbreak of war on the Rhine-Danube frontier compelled him to spend most of the next three years at Carnuntum. After successfully concluding his campaigns there by 174, he was called to Asia when his commander there, Avidius Cassius, revolted and declared himself emperor. Cassius, however, was murdered by his troops; the ever-magnanimous Marcus spurned the offer of his head and pardoned the Cassius family.

Faustina, Marcus's wife, died while accompanying him on his Asian tour; his grief appears to have been deeply felt. Returning to Rome through Athens, Marcus was initiated into the Eleusinian mysteries and endowed chairs of philosophy and rhetoric at the schools there. A year after his triumphal return to Rome in 176, renewed hostilities with German tribes forced Marcus to return to the Danube with his son. It was there, in the intervals of battle, that Marcus wrote down his *Meditations*, which he originally titled "To Himself," apparently intending them merely as a series of private reflections. He died at the military camp on March 17, 189, at the age of fifty-nine.

If the *Meditations* were simply another tract of mainstream Stoicism, it would likely not have emerged as a revered classic. It is precisely its unorthodox touches—its intimation of the idea of a personal god, its flashes of vulnerability and pain, its unwavering commitment to virtue above pleasure and to tranquillity above happiness, its unmistakable stamp of an uncompromisingly honest soul seeking the light of grace in a dark world—that lend the work its special power to charm and inspire. If at times Marcus's thoughts seem closer to Platonism or even Christianity than to Stoicism, we admire him all the more for grappling openly with the promptings of conscience rather than merely genuflecting before the dogmas of creed. A man who, for reasons of state, possibly sanctioned the persecution of Christians achieved a genuinely Christian depth of humility. In the words of Matthew Arnold, "What an affinity for Christianity had this persecutor of the Christians! The effusion of Christianity, its relieving tears, its happy self-sacrifice, were the very element, one feels, for which his soul longed; they were near him, they brushed him, he touched them, he passed them by."

Nearly two millennia after Marcus set down his thoughts, they speak with undiminished eloquence, giving us pause to wonder at a man who stood at the pinnacle of worldly power yet preserved the inner life of a saint.

A Note on the Translation

This edition of the *Meditations* is an updated and revised version of the George Long translation, much admired for its scrupulous fidelity to the ancient Greek text. To enhance readability, we have modernized some of the archaic language and tangled syntax of Long's Victorian prose, about which even his contemporary, Matthew Arnold, commented that it "is not quite idiomatic and simple enough." In a few passages, where Long's original formulations border on utter opacity, we have consulted the C. R. Haines translation for alternative renderings, taking care in all such cases to retain Long's equivalents for key concepts.

THE MEDITATIONS
OF
MARCUS AURELIUS ANTONINUS

BOOK I

From my grandfather Verus I learned good morals and the government of my temper.

2. From the reputation and remembrance of my father, modesty and a manly character.

3. From my mother, piety and beneficence, and abstinence, not only from evil deeds, but even from evil thoughts; and further, simplicity in my way of living, far removed from the habits of the rich.

4. From my great-grandfather, not to have frequented public schools, and to have good teachers at home, and to know that on such things a man should spend liberally.

5. From my governor, to be neither of the green nor of the blue party at the games in the Circus, nor a partisan either of the Parmularius or the Scutarius at the gladiators' fights; from him too I learned endurance of labor, and to want little, and to work with my own hands, and not to meddle with other people's affairs, and not to be ready to listen to slander.

6. From Diognetus, not to busy myself about trifling things, and not to give credit to what was said by miracle-workers and jugglers about incantations and the driving away of demons and such things; and not to breed quails for fighting, nor to give myself up passionately to such things; and to endure freedom of speech; and to have become intimate with philosophy; and to have been a hearer, first of Bacchius, then of Tandasis and Marcianus; and to have written dialogues in my youth; and to have desired a plank bed and skin, and whatever else of the kind belongs to the Grecian discipline.

1

7. From Rusticus I received the impression that my character required improvement and discipline; and from him I learned not to be led astray to sophistic emulation, nor to writing on speculative matters, nor to delivering little hortatory orations, nor to showing myself off as a man who practices much discipline, or does benevolent acts in order to make a display; and to abstain from rhetoric, and poetry, and fine writing; and not to walk about in the house in my outdoor dress, nor to do other things of the kind; and to write my letters with simplicity, like the letter that Rusticus wrote from Sinuessa to my mother; and with respect to those who have offended me by words, or done me wrong, to be easily disposed to be pacified and reconciled, as soon as they have shown a readiness to be reconciled; and to read carefully, and not to be satisfied with a superficial understanding of a book; nor hastily to give my assent to those who talk overmuch; and I am indebted to him for being acquainted with the discourses of Epictetus, which he communicated to me out of his own collection.

8. From Apollonius I learned freedom of will and undeviating steadiness of purpose; and to look to nothing else, not even for a moment, except to reason; and to be always the same, in sharp pains, on the occasion of the loss of a child, and in long illness; and to see clearly in a living example that the same man can be both most resolute and yielding, and not peevish in giving his instruction; and to have had before my eyes a man who clearly considered his experience and his skill in expounding philosophical principles as the smallest of his merits; and from him I learned how to receive from friends what are esteemed favors, without being either humbled by them or letting them pass unnoticed.

9. From Sextus, a benevolent disposition, and the example of a family governed in a fatherly manner, and the idea of living conformably to nature; and gravity without affectation, and to look carefully after the interest of friends, and to tolerate ignorant persons, and those who form opinions without consideration: he had the power of readily accommodating himself to all, so that intercourse with him was more agreeable than any flattery; and at the same time he was most highly venerated by those who associated with him; and he had the faculty both of discovering and ordering, in an intelligent and methodical way, the principles necessary for life; and he never showed anger or any other passion, but was entirely free from passion, and also most affectionate; and he could express approbation without noisy display, and he possessed much knowledge without ostentation.

10. From Alexander the grammarian, to refrain from fault-finding,

and not in a reproachful way to chide those who uttered any barbarous or solecistic or strange-sounding expression; but dexterously to introduce the very expression that ought to have been used, and in the way of answer or giving confirmation, or joining in an inquiry about the thing itself, not about the word, or by some other fit suggestion.

11. From Fronto I learned to observe what envy, and duplicity, and hypocrisy are in a tyrant, and that generally those among us who are called Patricians are rather deficient in paternal affection.

12. From Alexander the Platonic, not frequently nor without necessity to say to any one, or to write in a letter, that I have not leisure; nor continually to excuse the neglect of duties required by our relations to those with whom we live, by alleging urgent occupations.

13. From Catulus, not to be indifferent when a friend finds fault, even if he should find fault without reason, but to try to restore him to his usual disposition; and to be ready to speak well of teachers, as it is reported of Domitius and Athenodotus; and to love my children truly.

14. From my brother Severus, to love my kin, and to love truth, and to love justice; and through him I learned to know Thrasea, Helvidius, Cato, Dion, Brutus; and from him I received the idea of a polity in which there is the same law for all, a polity administered with regard to equal rights and equal freedom of speech, and the idea of a kingly government that respects most of all the freedom of the governed; I learned from him also consistency and undeviating steadiness in my regard for philosophy; and a disposition to do good, and to give to others readily, and to cherish good hopes, and to believe that I am loved by my friends; and in him I observed no concealment of his opinions with respect to those whom he condemned, and that his friends had no need to conjecture what he wished or did not wish, but it was quite plain.

15. From Maximus I learned self-government, and not to be led aside by anything; and cheerfulness in all circumstances, as well as in illness; and a just admixture in the moral character of sweetness and dignity, and to do what was set before me without complaining. I observed that everybody believed that he thought as he spoke, and that in all that he did he never had any bad intention; and he never showed amazement and surprise, and was never in a hurry, and never put off doing a thing, nor was perplexed nor dejected, nor did he ever laugh to disguise his vexation, nor, on the other hand, was he ever passionate or suspicious. He was accustomed to do acts of beneficence, and was ready to forgive, and was free from all falsehood; and he presented the appearance of a man who could not be diverted from right rather than

of a man who had been improved. I observed, too, that no man could ever think that he was despised by Maximus, or ever venture to think himself a better man. He had also the art of being humorous in an agreeable way.

16. In my adoptive father I observed mildness of temper, and unchangeable resolution in the things that he had determined after due deliberation; and no vainglory in those things that men call honors; and a love of labor and perseverance; and a readiness to listen to those who had anything to propose for the common weal; and undeviating firmness in giving to every man according to his deserts; and a knowledge derived from experience of the occasions for vigorous action and for remission. And I observed that he had overcome all passion for boys; and he considered himself no more than any other citizen; and he released his friends from all obligation to sup with him or to attend him of necessity when he went abroad, and those who had failed to accompany him, by reason of any urgent circumstances, always found him the same. I observed, too, his habit of careful inquiry in all matters of deliberation, and his persistency, and that he never stopped his investigation through being satisfied with appearances which first present themselves; and that his disposition was to keep his friends, and not to be soon tired of them, nor yet to be extravagant in his affection; and to be satisfied on all occasions, and cheerful; and to foresee things a long way off, and to provide for the smallest without display; and to check immediately popular applause and all flattery; and to be ever watchful over the things that were necessary for the administration of the empire, and to be a good manager of the expenditure, and patiently to endure the blame that he got for such conduct; and he was neither superstitious with respect to the gods, nor did he court men by gifts or by trying to please them, or by flattering the populace; but he showed sobriety in all things and firmness, and never any mean thoughts or actions, nor love of novelty. And the things that conduce in any way to the convenience of life, and of which fortune gives an abundant supply, he used without arrogance and without excusing himself; so that when he had them, he enjoyed them without affectation, and when he had them not, he did not want them. No one could ever say of him that he was either a sophist or a home-bred flippant slave or a pedant; but everyone acknowledged him to be a man ripe, perfect, above flattery, able to manage his own and other men's affairs. Besides this, he honored those who were true philosophers, and he did not reproach those who pretended to be philosophers, nor yet was he easily led by them. He was also easy in conversation, and he made himself agreeable with-

out any offensive affectation. He took a reasonable care of his body's health, not as one who was greatly attached to life, nor out of regard to personal appearance, nor yet in a careless way, but so that, through his own attention, he very seldom stood in need of the physician's art or of medicine or external applications. He was most ready to give way without envy to those who possessed any particular faculty, such as that of eloquence or knowledge of the law or of morals, or of anything else; and he gave them his help, that each might enjoy reputation according to his deserts; and he always acted conformably to the institutions of his country, without showing any affectation of doing so. Further, he was not fond of change nor unsteady, but he loved to stay in the same places, and to employ himself about the same things; and after his paroxysms of headache, he came immediately fresh and vigorous to his usual occupations. His secrets were not many, but very few and very rare, and these only about public matters; and he showed prudence and economy in the exhibition of the public spectacles and the construction of public buildings, in his donations to the people, and in all such things, for he was a man who looked to what ought to be done, not to the reputation that is got by a man's acts. He did not take the bath at unseasonable hours; he was not fond of building houses, nor curious about what he ate, nor about the texture and color of his clothes, nor about the beauty of his slaves. His dress came from Lorium, his villa on the coast, and from Lanuvium generally. We know how he behaved to the toll collector at Tusculum who asked his pardon; and such was all his behavior. There was in him nothing harsh, nor implacable, nor violent, nor, as one may say, anything carried to the sweating point; but he examined all things separately, as if he had abundance of time, and without confusion, in an orderly way, vigorously and consistently. And that might be applied to him which is recorded of Socrates, that he was able both to abstain from, and to enjoy, those things which many are too weak to abstain from, and cannot enjoy without excess. But to be strong enough both to bear the one and to be sober in the other is the mark of a man who has a perfect and invincible soul, such as he showed in the illness of Maximus.

17. To the gods I am indebted for having good grandfathers, good parents, a good sister, good teachers, good associates, good kinsmen and friends, nearly everything good. Further, I owe it to the gods that I was not hurried into any offense against any of them, though I had a disposition that, if opportunity had offered, might have led me to do something of this kind; but, through their favor, there never was such a concurrence of circumstances as put me to the trial. Further, I am

thankful to the gods that I was not longer brought up with my grandfather's concubine, and that I preserved the flower of my youth, and that I did not make proof of my virility before the proper season, but even deferred the time; that I was subjected to a ruler and a father who was able to take away all pride from me, and to bring me to the knowledge that it is possible for a man to live in a palace without desiring either guards or embroidered dresses, or torches and statues, and other such ostentation; but that it is in such a man's power to bring himself very near to the fashion of a private person, without being for this reason either meaner in thought, or more remiss in action, with respect to the things that must be done for the public interest in a manner that befits a ruler. I thank the gods for giving me such a brother, who was able by his moral character to rouse me to vigilance over myself, and who, at the same time, pleased me by his respect and affection; that my children have not been stupid nor deformed in body; that I did not make more proficiency in rhetoric, poetry, and the other studies, in which I should perhaps have been completely engaged, if I had seen that I was making progress in them; that I made haste to place those who brought me up in the station of honor, which they seemed to desire, without putting them off with hope of my doing it some time after, because they were then still young; that I knew Apollonius, Rusticus, Maximus; that I received clear and frequent impressions about living according to nature, and what kind of a life that is, so that, so far as depended on the gods, and their gifts, and help, and inspirations, nothing hindered me from forthwith living according to nature, though I still fall short of it through my own fault, and through not observing the admonitions of the gods, and, I may almost say, their direct instructions; that my body has held out so long in such a kind of life; that I never touched either Benedicta or Theodotus, and that, after having fallen into amatory passions, I was cured; and, though I was often out of humor with Rusticus, I never did anything of which I had occasion to repent; that, though it was my mother's fate to die young, she spent the last years of her life with me; that, whenever I wished to help any man in his need, or on any other occasion, I was never told that I had not the means of doing it; and that to myself the same necessity never happened, to receive anything from another; that I have such a wife, so obedient, and so affectionate, and so simple; that I had abundance of good masters for my children; and that remedies have been shown to me by dreams, both against other things, and against bloodspitting and giddiness; and that, when I had an inclination to philosophy, I did not fall into the hands of any sophist, and that I did not waste my time on writers of histories, or in the resolution of syllogisms, or occupy myself about the investigation of appearances in the heavens; for all these things require the help of the gods and fortune.

Among the Quadi at the Granua.

BOOK II

Begin the morning by saying to yourself, I shall meet with the busybody, the ungrateful, arrogant, deceitful, envious, unsocial. All these things happen to them by reason of their ignorance of what is good and evil. But I, who have seen the nature of the good that it is beautiful, and of the bad that it is ugly, and the nature of him who does wrong, that it is akin to me, not only of the same blood or seed, but that it participates in the same intelligence and the same portion of the divinity, I can neither be injured by any of them, for no one can fix on me what is ugly, nor can I be angry with my kinsman, nor hate him. For we are made for cooperation, like feet, like hands, like eyelids, like the rows of the upper and lower teeth. To act against one another then is contrary to nature; and it is acting against one another to be vexed and to turn away.

2. Whatever this is that I am, it is a little flesh and breath, and the ruling part. Throw away your books; no longer distract yourself: it is not allowed; but as if you were now dying, despise the flesh; it is blood and bones and a network, a contexture of nerves, veins, and arteries. See the breath also, what kind of a thing it is, air, and not always the same, but every moment sent out and again sucked in. The third then is the ruling part—consider thus: You are an old man; no longer let this be a slave, no longer be pulled by the strings like a puppet to unsocial movements, no longer be either dissatisfied with your present lot, or shrink from the future.

3. All that is from the gods is full of Providence. Even that which is from chance is not separated from nature or without an interweaving and involution with the things that are ordered by Providence. From thence all things flow; and there is also necessity, and that which is for the advantage of the whole universe, of which you are a part. But what the nature of the whole brings is good for every part of nature, and serves to maintain it. Now the universe is preserved, as by the changes of the elements so by the changes of things compounded of the elements. Let these principles be enough for you, let them always be fixed opinions. But cast away the thirst after books, that you might not die

8

grumbling, but cheerfully, truly, and from your heart thankful to the gods.

4. Remember how long you have been putting off these things, and how often you have received an opportunity from the gods, and yet do not use it. You must now at last perceive of what universe you are a part, and from what administrator of the universe your existence flows, and that a limit of time is fixed for you, which if you do not use for clearing away the clouds from your mind, it will go and you will go, and it will never return.

5. Every moment think steadily as a Roman and a man to do what you have in hand with perfect and simple dignity and feeling of affection and freedom and justice; and to give yourself relief from all other thoughts. And you will give yourself relief, if you do every act of your life as if it were the last, laying aside all carelessness, passionate aversion from the commands of reason, hypocrisy, self-love, and discontent with the portion that has been given to you. You see how few the things are, which if possessed by a man, enable him to live a life that flows in quiet, and is like the existence of the gods; for the gods on their part will require nothing more from him who observes these things.

6. Wrong yourself, wrong yourself, my soul; but you will not much longer have the chance to honor yourself. Every man's life is sufficient. But yours is nearly finished, and still your soul reveres not itself, but seeks your well-being in the souls of others.

7. Do the external things that fall upon you distract you? Give yourself time to learn something new and good, and cease to be whirled around. But then you must also avoid being carried about the other way. For those, too, are triflers who have wearied themselves in life by their activity and yet have no object to which to direct every movement and every thought.

8. Failure to observe what is in the mind of another has seldom made a man unhappy; but those who do not observe the movements of their own minds must of necessity be unhappy.

9. This you must always bear in mind, what is the nature of the whole, and what is my nature, and how this is related to that, and what kind of a part it is of what kind of a whole; and that there is no one who hinders you from always doing and saying the things that conform to the nature of which you are a part.

10. Theophrastus, in his comparison of bad acts—such a comparison as one would make in accordance with the common notions of mankind—says, like a true philosopher, that offenses committed through desire are more blamable than those committed through

anger. For he who is excited by anger seems to turn away from reason with a certain pain and unconscious contraction; but he who offends through desire, being overpowered by pleasure, seems more intemperate and more womanish in his offenses. Rightly then, and in a way worthy of philosophy, he said that the offense committed with pleasure is more blamable than that committed with pain; and on the whole the one is more like a person who has been first wronged and through pain is compelled to be angry; but the other is moved by his own impulse to do wrong, being carried toward doing something by desire.

11. Since it is possible that you might depart from life this very moment, regulate every act and thought accordingly. But to go away from among men, if there are gods, is not a thing to be afraid of, for the gods will not involve you in evil; but if indeed they do not exist, or if they have no concern about human affairs, why would I wish to live in a universe devoid of gods or devoid of Providence? But in truth they do exist, and they do care for human things, and they have put all the means in man's power to enable him not to fall into real evils. And as to the rest, if there were anything evil, they would have provided that it should be altogether in a man's power not to fall into it. Now that which does not make a man worse, how can it make a man's life worse? But neither through ignorance nor having the knowledge but not the power to guard against or correct these things, is it possible that the nature of the universe has overlooked them; nor is it possible that it has made so great mistake, either through want of power or skill, that good and evil should happen indiscriminately to the good and the bad. But death and life, honor and dishonor, pain and pleasure—all these things equally happen to good men and bad, being things which make us neither better nor worse. Therefore they are neither good nor evil.

12. How quickly all things disappear: in the universe the bodies themselves, but in time the memory of them; what is the nature of all sensible things, and particularly those that attract with the bait of pleasure or terrify by pain, or are noised abroad by vapory fame; how worthless and contemptible and sordid and perishable and dead they are— all this it is the part of the intellectual faculty to observe. To observe, too, those whose opinions and voices give reputation; what death is, and the fact that if a man looks at it in itself, and by the abstractive power of reflection resolves into their parts all the things that present themselves to the imagination in it, he will then consider it to be nothing else than an operation of nature; and if any one is afraid of an operation of nature, he is a child. This, however, is not only an operation of nature, but it is also a thing that conduces to the purposes of nature. To

observe, too, how man comes near to the deity, and by what part of him, and when this part of man is so disposed.

13. Nothing is more wretched than a man who traverses everything in a round, and pries into the things beneath the earth, as the poet says, and seeks by conjecture what is in the minds of his neighbors, without perceiving that it is sufficient to attend to the daimon within him and to revere it sincerely. And reverence of the daimon consists in keeping it pure from passion and thoughtlessness, and dissatisfaction with what comes from gods and men. For the things from the gods merit veneration for their excellence; and the things from men should be dear to us by reason of kinship; and sometimes even, in a manner, they move our pity by reason of men's ignorance of good and bad, a defect akin to an inability to distinguish things that are white and black.

14. Even if you were going to live three thousand years, and even ten thousand times that, still remember that no man loses any other life than this which he now lives, nor lives any other than this which he now loses. The longest and shortest are thus brought to the same. For the present is the same to all, though that which perishes is not the same; and so what is lost appears to be a mere moment. For a man cannot lose either the past or the future: for what a man has not, how can anyone take this from him? These two things then you must bear in mind: the one, that all things from eternity are of like forms and come round in a circle, and that it makes no difference whether a man shall see the same things during a hundred years or two hundred, or an infinite time; and the second, that he who lives longest and he who will die soonest lose just the same. For the present is the only thing of which a man can be deprived, if it is true that this is the only thing which he has, and that a man cannot lose something he does not already possess.

15. There is obvious truth to the statement by the Cynic Monimus that "all is opinion." And obvious, too, is the usefulness of this statement if a man profits from it insofar as it is true.

16. The soul of man does violence to itself, first of all, when it becomes an abscess and, as it were, a tumor on the universe. For to be vexed at anything that happens is a separation of ourselves from nature, in some part of which the natures of all other things are contained. In the next place, the soul does violence to itself when it turns away from any man, or even moves toward him with the intention of injuring, as happens when people are angry. In the third place, the soul does violence to itself when it is overpowered by pleasure or by pain. Fourth, when it playacts and does or says anything insincerely and untruly. Fifth, when it allows any act of its own and any movement to be with-

out an aim and does anything thoughtlessly and without considering
what it is — even the smallest things should be done with reference to
an end; and the end of rational animals is to follow the reason and the
law of the most ancient city and polity.

17. In human life time is but an instant, and the substance of it a
flux, and the perception dull, and the composition of the whole body
subject to putrefaction, and the soul a whirl, and fortune hard to divine,
and fame a thing devoid of certainty. And, to say all in a word, everything that belongs to the body is a stream, and what belongs to the soul
is a dream and vapor, and life is a warfare and a stranger's sojourn, and
after-fame is oblivion. What then can guide a man? One thing and only
one, philosophy. But this consists in keeping the daimon within a man
free from violence and unharmed, superior to pains and pleasures,
doing nothing without a purpose, nor yet falsely and with hypocrisy,
not feeling the need of another man's doing or not doing anything; and
besides, accepting all that happens, and all that is allotted, as coming
from the same source, wherever it is, from which he himself came;
and, finally, waiting for death with a cheerful mind, as being nothing
else than a dissolution of the elements of which every living being is
compounded. But if there is no harm to the elements themselves in
each continually changing into another, why should a man have any
apprehension about the change and dissolution of all the elements? For
it is according to nature, and nothing is evil that is according to nature.

This in Carnuntum.

BOOK III

We ought to consider not only that our life is daily wasting away and a smaller part of it is left, but also that if a man should live longer, it is quite uncertain whether the understanding will still continue sufficient for the comprehension of things and retain the power of contemplation that strives to acquire the knowledge of the divine and the human. For if he shall begin to fall into dotage, perspiration and nutrition and imagination and appetite and whatever else there is of the kind will not fail; but the power of making use of ourselves, and filling up the measure of our duty, and clearly separating all appearances, and considering whether a man should now depart from life, and whatever else of the kind absolutely requires a disciplined reason, all this is already extinguished. We must make haste then, not only because we are daily nearer to death, but also because the conception of things and the understanding of them cease first.

2. We ought to observe also that even the things which follow after the things that are produced according to nature contain something pleasing and attractive. For instance, when bread is baked, some parts are split at the surface, and these parts which thus open, and have a certain fashion contrary to the purpose of the baker's art, are beautiful in a manner, and in a peculiar way excite a desire for eating. And again, figs, when they are quite ripe, gape open; and in the ripe olives the very circumstance of their being near to rottenness adds a peculiar beauty to the fruit. And the ears of corn bending down, and the lion's eyebrows, and the foam that flows from the mouth of wild boars, and many other things—though they are far from being beautiful, if a man should examine them separately—still, because they follow from the things that are formed by nature, help to adorn them, and they please the mind; so that if a man should have a feeling and deeper insight with respect to the things that are produced in the universe, there is hardly one of those by-products that will not fail to give pleasure. And so he will see even the real gaping jaws of wild beasts with no less pleasure than those that painters and sculptors show by imitation; and in an old

woman and an old man he will be able to see a certain maturity and
comeliness; and the attractive loveliness of young persons he will be
able to look on with chaste eyes; and many such things will seem pleasing, but only to him who has become truly familiar with nature and her
works.

3. Hippocrates, after curing many diseases, himself fell sick and died.
The Chaldaie foretold the deaths of many, and then fate caught them,
too. Alexander and Pompeius and Gaius Caesar, after so often completely destroying whole cities, and in battle cutting to pieces many ten
thousands of cavalry and infantry, themselves, too, at last departed from
life. Heraclitus, after so many speculations on the conflagration of the
universe, was filled with water and died smeared all over with cow
dung. And lice destroyed Democritus; and other lice killed Socrates.
What does all this mean? You have embarked, made the voyage, and
come to shore; get out. If indeed to another life, there is no want of
gods, not even there. But if to a state without sensation, you will cease
to be held by pains and pleasures, and to be a slave to the vessel, which
is as much inferior as that which serves it is superior: for the one is intelligence and deity; the other is earth and corruption.

4. Do not waste the remainder of your life in thoughts about others,
when you do not refer your thoughts to some object of common utility. For you lose the opportunity of doing something else when you have
such thoughts as these. What is such a person doing, and why, and
what is he saying, and what is he thinking of, and what is he contriving,
and whatever else of the kind makes us wander away from the observation of our own ruling power. We ought then to check in the series of
our thoughts everything that is without a purpose and useless, but most
of all the overcurious feeling and the malignant; and a man should use
himself to think of those things only about which if one should suddenly ask, What are you thinking about? With perfect openness you
might immediately answer, this or that; so that from your words it
should be plain that everything in you is simple and benevolent, as
befits a social animal, one that is unconcerned with pleasure, sensual
enjoyments, rivalry, envy, suspicion, or any other thoughts that you
would blush to admit. When such a man comes to the fore, he is like
a priest and minister of the gods, guided by the deity within that
makes the man uncontaminated by pleasure, unharmed by any pain,
untouched by any insult, feeling no wrong, a fighter in the noblest
fight, one who cannot be overpowered by any passion, dyed deep with
justice, accepting with all his soul everything that happens and is
assigned to him as his portion; and only with great necessity and for the

general interest imagining what another says or does or thinks. For his activity concentrates on his own lot; and he constantly thinks of that portion of things that has been allotted to him, and he makes his own acts fair, and he is persuaded that his own portion is good. For the lot that is assigned to each man is carried along with him and carries him along with it. And he remembers also that every rational animal is his kinsman, and that to care for all men is according to man's nature; and a man should value the opinion only of those who openly live according to nature. But as to those who do not, he always bears in mind what kind of men they are both at home and from home, both by night and by day, and what they are, and with what men they live an impure life. Accordingly, he does not value at all the praise that comes from such men, since they are not even satisfied with themselves.

5. Labor willingly and diligently, undistracted and aware of the common interest; do not let studied ornament set off your thoughts, and be not either a man of many words or busy about too many things. And further, let the deity within you be the guardian of a living being, manly and of ripe age, and engaged in matters political, and a Roman, and a ruler, who has taken his post like a man waiting for the signal that summons him from life, and ready to go, having need neither of oath nor of any man's testimony. Be cheerful also, and do not seek external help or the tranquillity that others give. A man then must stand erect, not be kept erect by others.

6. If you find in human life anything better than justice, truth, temperance, fortitude, anything better than your own mind's self-satisfaction in the things that it enables you to do according to right reason, and in the condition that is assigned to you without your own choice; if, I say, you see anything better than this, turn to it with all your soul, and enjoy that which you have found to be the best. But if nothing appears to be better than the deity that is planted in you, that has power over your appetites, and carefully examines all the impressions, and, as Socrates said, has detached itself from the persuasions of sense, has submitted itself to the gods, and cares for mankind; if you find everything else smaller and of less value than this, give place to nothing else, for if you diverge from this deity and succumb to the appetites, you will no longer be able to concentrate on that good thing that is most deeply your own; for it is not right that anything of any other kind, such as praise from the many, or power, or enjoyment of pleasure, should come into competition with that which is rationally and politically or practically good. Although these distractions may seem to adapt themselves to the better things in a small degree, they in fact subjugate reason all

at once and carry us away. Simply and freely choose the better, and hold to it. The better is that which is useful to you as a rational being; but if something is only useful to you as an animal, say so, and maintain your judgment without arrogance: only take care that you make the inquiry by a sure method.

7. Never value anything as profitable that compels you to break your promise, to lose your self-respect, to hate any man, to suspect, to curse, to act the hypocrite, to desire anything that needs walls and curtains: for he who has preferred to everything else his own intelligence and daimon and the worship of its excellence, acts no tragic part, does not groan, will not need either solitude or much company; and, what is chief of all, he will live without either pursuing or flying from death; but whether for a longer or a shorter time he shall have the soul enclosed in the body, he cares not at all: for even if he must depart immediately, he will go as readily as if he were going to do anything else that can be done with decency and order; taking care of this only all through life, that his thoughts abide with the concerns of an intelligent animal and a member of a civil community.

8. In the mind of one who is chastened and purified you will find no corrupt matter, impurity, or any sore skinned over. Nor is his life incomplete when fate overtakes him, as one may say of an actor who leaves the stage before ending and finishing the play. Besides, there is in him nothing servile or affected, too closely bound to other things or yet detached from other things, nothing worthy of blame, nothing that seeks a hiding place.

9. Revere the faculty that produces opinion. This faculty determines whether there shall exist in your ruling part any opinion inconsistent with nature and the constitution of the rational animal. And this faculty promises freedom from hasty judgment, friendship toward men, and obedience to the gods.

10. Casting aside other things, hold to the precious few; and besides bear in mind that every man lives only the present, which is an indivisible point, and that all the rest of his life is either past or is uncertain. Brief is man's life and small the nook of the earth where he lives; brief, too, is the longest posthumous fame, buoyed only by a succession of poor human beings who will very soon die and who know little of themselves, much less of someone who died long ago.

11. To the aids that have been mentioned let this one still be added: Make for yourself a definition or description of the thing that is presented to you, so as to see distinctly what kind of a thing it is in its substance, in its nudity, in its entirety, and tell yourself its proper name and

the names of the things of which it has been compounded and into which it will be resolved. For nothing so promotes elevation of mind as the ability to examine methodically and truly every object that is presented to you in life, and always to look at things so as to see at the same time what kind of universe this is, and what kind of use everything performs in it, and what value everything has with reference to the whole, and what with reference to man, who is a citizen of the highest city, of which all other cities are like families; what each thing is, its composition and duration, and what virtue I need bring to it, such as gentleness, manliness, truth, fidelity, simplicity, contentment, and the rest. On every occasion a man should be able to say: this comes from God; and this is according to the apportionment and spinning of the thread of destiny, coincidence, or chance; and this is from someone of the same stock, a kinsman and partner, but one who is ignorant of what is really in accordance with his nature. But I know; for this reason I behave towards him according to the natural law of fellowship, with benevolence and justice. At the same time, however, in things neither good nor bad I attempt to ascertain the value of each.

12. If you apply yourself to the task before you, following right reason seriously, vigorously, calmly, without allowing anything else to distract you, but keeping your divine part pure, as if you might be bound to give it back immediately; if you hold to this, expecting nothing, fearing nothing, but satisfied with your present activities according to nature, and with heroic truth in every word and sound which you utter, you will live happily. And there is no man who is able to prevent this.

13. As physicians have always their instruments and knives ready for cases that suddenly require their skill, so do you have principles ready for the understanding of things divine and human, and for doing everything, even the smallest, with a recollection of the bond that unites the divine and human to each other. For neither can you do anything well that pertains to man without at the same time having a reference to things divine; nor the contrary.

14. No longer wander at hazard; for neither will you read your own memoirs, nor the acts of the ancient Romans and Hellenes, and the selections from books you were reserving for your old age. Hasten then to your appointed end and, throwing away idle hopes, come to your own aid, if you care at all for yourself, while it is in your power.

15. They know not how many things are signified by the words *stealing, sowing, buying, keeping quiet, seeing what ought to be done*; for this is not effected by the eyes, but by another kind of vision.

16. Body, soul, intelligence: to the body belong sensations, to the

soul appetites, to the intelligence principles. To receive the impressions of forms by means of appearances belongs even to animals; to be pulled by the strings of desire belongs to wild beasts, effeminate men, a Phalaris, or a Nero; and the intelligence that guides one to the things that appear suitable belongs also to those who do not believe in the gods, who betray their country, and do their impure deeds when they have shut the doors. If then everything else is common to all that I have mentioned, there remains that which is peculiar to the good man, to be pleased and content with what happens, and with the thread that is spun for him; and not to defile the divinity that is planted in his breast, nor disturb it by a crowd of images, but to preserve it tranquilly, following it obediently as a god, neither saying anything contrary to the truth nor doing anything contrary to justice. And if all men refuse to believe that he lives a simple, modest, and contented life, he is neither angry with any of them, nor does he deviate from the way that leads to the end of life, to which a man ought to come pure, tranquil, ready to depart, and without any compulsion, perfectly reconciled to his lot.

BOOK IV

That which rules within, when it is according to nature, will always adapt itself easily to that which is possible and is presented to it. For it requires no definite material, in moving toward its purpose, but rather certain conditions; and it makes a material for itself out of that which opposes it, as a great fire lays hold of a mass that would have extinguished a tiny flame: when the fire is strong, it soon appropriates to itself the matter that is heaped on it and consumes it, rising higher by means of this very material.

2. Let no act be done without a purpose, nor otherwise than according to the perfect principles of art.

3. Men seek retreats for themselves, houses in the country, seashores, and mountains; and you, too, are wont to desire such things very much. But this is altogether a mark of the most common sort of men, for it is in your power whenever you choose to retire into yourself. For there is no retreat that is quieter or freer from trouble than a man's own soul, especially when he has within him such thoughts that by looking into them he is immediately in perfect tranquillity; and tranquillity is nothing else than the good ordering of the mind. Constantly then give to yourself this retreat, and renew yourself; and let your principles be brief and fundamental, which, as soon as you recur to them, will be sufficient to cleanse the soul completely, and to send you back free from all discontent with the things to which you return.

For with what are you discontented? With the badness of men? Recall to your mind this conclusion, that rational animals exist for one another, and that to endure is a part of justice, and that men do wrong involuntarily; and consider how many already, after mutual enmity, suspicion, hatred, and fighting, have been stretched dead, reduced to ashes; and be quiet at last. But perhaps you are dissatisfied with that which is assigned to you out of the universe. Recall the alternative; either there is providence or a fortuitous concurrence of atoms; or remember the arguments by which it has been proved that the world is a kind of political community, and be quiet at last. But perhaps corpo-

19

real things will still fasten upon you. Consider then further that once
the mind has drawn itself apart and discovered its own power, it no
longer mingles with the breath, whether moving gently or violently,
and think also of all that you have heard and assented to about pain and
pleasure, and be quiet at last.

But perhaps the desire of the thing called fame torments you. See
how soon everything is forgotten, and look at the chaos of infinite time
on each side of the present, and the emptiness of applause, and the
fickleness and lack of judgment in those who pretend to give praise,
and the narrowness of its domain, and be quiet at last. For the whole
earth is a point, and how small a nook in it is this your dwelling, and
how few are there in it, and what kind of people are they who will
praise thee.

This then remains: Remember to retire into this little territory of
your own, and above all do not distract or strain yourself, but be free,
and look at things as a man, as a human being, as a citizen, as a mortal. But among the things readiest to hand to which you should turn,
let there be these two: One is that things do not touch the soul, for they
are external and remain immovable; so our perturbations come only
from our inner opinions. The other is that all the things you see around
you change immediately and will no longer be; and constantly bear in
mind how many of these changes you have already witnessed. The universe is transformation: life is opinion.

4. If the intellectual is common to all men, so is reason, in respect of
which we are rational beings: if this is so, common also is the reason
that commands us what to do, and what not to do; if this is so, there is
a common law also; if this is so, we are fellow-citizens; if this is so, we
are members of some political community; if this is so, the world is in
a manner a state. For of what other common political community will
anyone say that the whole human race are members? And from this
common political community comes also our very intellectual faculty
and reasoning faculty and our capacity for law; where else could they
come from? For as my earthly part comes from the earth, and the
watery part from another element, and that which is hot and fiery from
some peculiar source (for nothing comes out of nothing, as nothing
also returns to nonexistence), so also the intellectual part comes from
some source.

5. Death, like generation, is a mystery of nature; a composition out
of the same elements, and a decomposition into the same; and altogether not a thing of which any man should be ashamed, for it is not

contrary to the nature of a reasonable animal, and not contrary to the reason of our constitution.

6. It is natural that certain things should be done by a certain kind of person; it is a matter of necessity. And if a man will not have it so, he will not allow the fig tree to have juice. But by all means bear this in mind, that within a very short time both you and he will be dead; and soon not even your names will be left behind.

7. Take away your opinion, and then there is taken away the complaint, "I have been harmed." Take away the complaint, "I have been harmed," and the harm is taken away.

8. That which does not make a man worse than he was, also does not make his life worse, nor does it harm him either from without or from within.

9. The nature of that which is universally useful has been compelled to do this.

10. Note that everything that happens, happens justly, and if you observe carefully, you will find it to be so, not only with respect to the continuity of the series of things, but with respect to what is just, as if it were done by one who assigns to each thing its value. Observe then as you have begun; and whatever you do, do it in conjunction with goodness, in the sense in which a man is properly understood to be good. Keep to this in every action.

11. Do not have such an opinion of things as he has who does you wrong, or such as he wishes you to have, but look at them as they are in truth.

12. A man should always have these two rules in readiness: one, to do only whatever the reason of the ruling and legislating faculty may suggest for the use of men; the other, to change your opinion, if anyone sets you right and dissuades you from any opinion. But this change of opinion must proceed only from a genuine conviction about what is just or of common advantage, and the like, not because it appears pleasant or brings reputation.

13. Do you have reason? I have. Why then do you not use it? For if reason does its own work, what else could you wish for?

14. You have existed as a part. You shall disappear in that which produced you; or rather you shall be received back into its seminal principle by transmutation.

15. Many grains of frankincense on the same altar: one falls before, another falls after; but it makes no difference.

16. Within ten days you will seem a god to those to whom you are

now a beast and an ape, if you will return to your principles and the worship of reason.

17. Do not act as if you were going to live ten thousand years. Death hangs over you. While you live, while it is in your power, be good.

18. How much trouble he avoids who does not look to see what his neighbor says or does or thinks, but only to what he does himself, that it may be just and pure; or as Agathon says, look not round at the depraved morals of others, but run straight along the line without deviating from it.

19. He who has a vehement desire for posthumous fame does not consider that every one of those who remember him will himself also die very soon; then again also they who have succeeded them, until the whole remembrance shall have been extinguished as it is transmitted through men who foolishly admire and perish. But suppose that those who will remember are even immortal, and that the remembrance will be immortal, what then is this to you? And I say not what is it to the dead, but what is it to the living? What is praise except indeed so far as it has a certain utility? For you now reject unseasonably the gift of nature, clinging to something else. . . .

20. Everything that is in any way beautiful is beautiful in itself and terminates in itself, not having praise as part of itself since a thing is neither better nor worse for having been praised. I affirm this also of the things that are called beautiful by the vulgar, for example, material things and works of art. That which is really beautiful has no need of anything; not more than law, not more than truth, not more than benevolence or modesty. Which of these things is beautiful because it is praised, or spoiled by being blamed? Is such a thing as an emerald made worse than it was, if it is not praised? Or gold, ivory, purple, a lyre, a little knife, a flower, a shrub?

21. If souls continue to exist, how does the air contain them from eternity? But how does the earth contain the bodies of those who have been buried from time so remote? For as here the mutation of these bodies after a certain continuance, whatever it may be, and their dissolution make room for other dead bodies; so the souls that are removed into the air after subsisting for some time are transmuted and diffused, and assume a fiery nature by being received into the seminal intelligence of the universe, and in this way make room for the fresh souls that come to dwell there. And this is the answer that a man might give on the hypothesis of souls continuing to exist. But we must not only think of the number of bodies that are thus buried, but also of the number of animals that are daily eaten by us and the other animals. For what a number is consumed, and thus in a manner buried in the bod-

ies of those who feed on them! And nevertheless this earth receives them by reason of the changes of these bodies into blood, and the transformations into the aerial or the fiery element.

How can we arrive at the truth in this matter? By a division into that which is material and that which is the cause of form, the formal.

22. Do not be whirled about, but in every movement have respect to justice, and on the occasion of every impression maintain the faculty of comprehension or understanding.

23. Everything harmonizes with me, which is harmonious to you, O Universe. For me nothing is too early or too late if it is in due time for you. Everything is fruit to me that your seasons bring, O Nature: from you are all things, in you are all things, to you all things return. The poet says, Dear city of Cecrops; and will you not say, Dear city of Zeus?

24. Occupy yourself with few things, says the philosopher, if you would be tranquil. But consider if it would not be better to say, Do what is necessary, and whatever the reason of a social animal naturally requires, and as it requires. For this brings not only the tranquillity that comes from doing well, but also that which comes from doing few things. Since the greatest part of what we say and do is unnecessary, dispensing with such activities affords a man more leisure and less uneasiness. Accordingly on every occasion a man should ask himself, Is this one of the unnecessary things? Now a man should take away not only unnecessary acts, but also unnecessary thoughts so that superfluous acts will not follow after.

25. See how the life of the good man suits you, the life of him who is satisfied with his portion of the whole, and satisfied with his own just acts and benevolent disposition.

26. Have you seen those things? Look also at these. Do not disturb yourself. Make yourself all simplicity. Does anyone do wrong? It is to himself that he does the wrong. Has anything happened to you? Well, out of the universe from the beginning everything that happens has been apportioned and spun out to you. In a word, your life is short. You must turn to profit the present by the aid of reason and justice. Be sober in your relaxation.

27. Either it is a well-arranged universe or a chaos huddled together, but still a universe. But can a certain order subsist in you and disorder in the All? And this, too, when all things are so separated and diffused and sympathetic.

28. A black character, a womanish character, a stubborn character, bestial, childish, animal, stupid, counterfeit, scurrilous, fraudulent, tyrannical.

29. If he is a stranger to the universe who does not know what is in

it, no less is he a stranger who does not know what is going on in it. He is a runaway, who flies from social reason; he is blind, who shuts the eyes of the understanding; he is poor, who has need of another, and has not from himself all things that are useful for life. He is an abscess on the universe who withdraws and separates himself from the reason of our common nature through being displeased with the things that happen; for the same nature that produces these things has produced you, too: he is a piece rent asunder from the state, who tears his own soul from that of the unitary soul of all rational beings.

30. The one is a philosopher without a tunic, and the other without a book: here is another half naked: Bread I have not, he says, and I abide by reason. And I do not get the means of living out of my learning, yet I abide by my reason.

31. Love the art, poor as it may be, that you have learned, and be content with it; and pass through the rest of life like one who has entrusted to the gods with his whole soul all that he has, making yourself neither the tyrant nor the slave of any man.

32. Consider, for example, the times of Vespasian. You will see all these things, people marrying, bringing up children, sick, dying, warring, feasting, trafficking, cultivating the ground, flattering, obstinately arrogant, suspecting, plotting, wishing for some to die, grumbling about the present, loving, heaping up treasure, desiring consulship, kingly power. Well then, that life of these people no longer exists at all. Again, remove to the times of Trajan. Again, all is the same. Their life, too, is gone. In like manner view also the other epochs of time and of whole nations, and see how many after great efforts soon fell and were resolved into the elements. But chiefly you should think of those whom you have yourself known distracting themselves about idle things rather than acting in accordance with their proper constitution, holding firmly to this and remaining content with it. And herein it is necessary to remember that the attention given to everything has its proper value and proportion. For you will not be dissatisfied if you apply yourself to smaller matters no further than is fit.

33. Once familiar words are now antiquated, as are the names of those who were famed of old: Camillus, Caeso, Volesus, Leonnatus, and a little later also Scipio and Cato, then Augustus, then also Hadrian and Antoninus. For all things soon pass away and become a mere tale, and complete oblivion soon buries them. And I say this of those who have shone in a wondrous way. For the rest, as soon as they have breathed out their breath, they are gone, and no man speaks of them. And, to conclude the matter, what is even an eternal remembrance? A mere nothing. What then is that about which we ought to employ our

serious pains? This one thing, just thoughts, and social acts, and words that never lie, and a disposition that gladly accepts all that happens as necessary, as usual, as flowing from a principle and source of the same kind.

34. Willingly give yourself up to Clotho, one of the Fates, allowing her to spin your thread into whatever things she pleases.

35. Everything is only for a day, both that which remembers and that which is remembered.

36. Observe constantly that all things take place by change, and accustom yourself to consider that the nature of the universe loves nothing so much as to change the things that are and to make new things like them. For everything that exists is in a manner the seed of that which will be. But you are thinking only of seeds that are cast into the earth or into a womb: but this is a very vulgar notion.

37. You will soon die, and you are not yet simple, not free from perturbations, nor without suspicion of being hurt by external things, nor kindly disposed toward all; nor do you yet realize that acting justly is the only true wisdom.

38. Examine men's ruling principles, even those of the wise, what kind of things they avoid, and what kind they pursue.

39. What is evil to you does not subsist in the ruling principle of another; nor yet in any turning and mutation of your corporeal covering. Where is it then? It is in that part of you in which subsists the power of forming opinions about evils. Let this power then not form such opinions, and all is well. And if that which is nearest to it, the poor body, is cut, burned, filled with matter and rottenness, nevertheless let the part that forms opinions about these things be quiet, that is, let it judge that nothing is either bad or good that can happen equally to the bad man and the good. For that which happens equally to him who lives contrary to nature and to him who lives according to nature, is neither according to nature nor contrary to nature.

40. Constantly regard the universe as one living being, having one substance and one soul; and observe how all things have reference to one perception, the perception of this one living being; and how all things act with one movement; and how all things are the cooperating causes of all things that exist; observe, too, the continuous spinning of the thread and the contexture of the web.

41. You are a little soul bearing up a corpse, as Epictetus used to say.

42. It is no evil for things to undergo change, and no good for things to subsist in consequence of change.

43. Time is like a river made up of the events that happen, and a vio-

lent stream; for as soon as a thing has been seen, it is carried away, and another comes in its place, and this will be carried away, too.

44. Everything that happens is as familiar and well known as the rose in spring and the fruit in summer; for such is disease and death and calumny and treachery and whatever else delights fools or vexes them.

45. In the series of things, those that follow are always aptly fitted to those that have gone before; for this series is not like a mere enumeration of disjointed things, which has only a necessary sequence, but it is a rational connection: and as all existing things are arranged together harmoniously, so the things that come into existence exhibit no mere succession but a certain wonderful relationship.

46. Always remember the saying of Heraclitus, that the death of earth is to become water, and the death of water is to become air, and the death of air is to become fire, and reversely. And think, too, of him who forgets whither the way leads, and that men quarrel with that with which they are most constantly in communion, the reason that governs the universe; and the things that they daily meet with seem to them strange: and consider that we ought not to act and speak as if we were asleep, for even in sleep we seem to act and speak; and that we ought not, like children who learn from their parents, simply to act and speak as we have been taught.

47. If any god told you that you will die tomorrow, or certainly on the day after tomorrow, you would not care much whether it was on the third day or on the morrow, unless you were in the highest degree mean-spirited—for how small is the difference? So think it no great thing to die after as many years as you can name rather than tomorrow.

48. Think continually how many physicians are dead after often contracting their eyebrows over the sick; and how many astrologers after predicting with great pretensions the deaths of others; and how many philosophers after endless discourses on death or immortality; how many heroes after killing thousands; and how many tyrants who have used their power over men's lives with terrible insolence as if they were immortal; and how many cities are entirely dead—for example, Helice and Pompeii and Herculaneum and others innumerable. Add to the reckoning all those you have known, one after another. One man after burying another has been laid out dead, and another buries him: and all this in a short time. To conclude, always observe how ephemeral and worthless human things are, and what was yesterday a speck of semen tomorrow will be a mummy or ashes. Pass then through this little space of time conformably to nature, and end your journey in con-

tent, just as an olive falls off when it is ripe, blessing nature who produced it and thanking the tree on which it grew.

49.´ Be like the promontory against which the waves continually break; but it stands firm and tames the fury of the water around it.

"I am unhappy, because this has happened to me." Not so: say, "I am happy, though this has happened to me, because I continue free from pain, neither crushed by the present nor fearing the future." For such a thing as this might have happened to every man; but every man would not have continued free from pain on such an occasion. Why then is that rather a misfortune than this a good fortune? And do you in all cases define as a misfortune that which is not a deviation from man's nature? And does a thing seem to you to be a deviation from man's nature if it is not contrary to the will of man's nature? Well, you know the will of nature. Will this that has happened prevent you from being just, magnanimous, temperate, prudent, secure against inconsiderate opinions and falsehood; will it prevent you from having modesty, freedom, and everything else, by the presence of which man's nature obtains all that is its own? Remember, too, on every occasion that leads you to vexation to apply this principle: not that this is a misfortune, but that to bear it nobly is good fortune.

50. It is a vulgar but still a useful help toward contempt of death to pass in review those who have tenaciously stuck to life. What more have they gained than those who have died early? Certainly they lie in their tombs somewhere at last, Cadicianus, Fabius, Julianus, Lepidus, or any one else like them, who have carried out many to be buried and then were carried out themselves. Altogether the interval is small between birth and death; and consider with how much trouble, and in company with what sort of people and in what a feeble body, this interval is laboriously passed. Do not then consider life a thing of any value. For look to the immensity of time behind you and to the time that is ahead of you, another boundless space. In this infinity, then, what is the difference between him who lives three days and him who lives three generations?

51. Always run to the short way; and the short way is natural: accordingly say and do everything in conformity with the soundest reason. For such a purpose frees a man from trouble, and warfare, and all artifice and ostentatious display.

BOOK V

In the morning, when you rise unwillingly, let this thought be present: I am rising to the work of a human being. Why then am I dissatisfied if I am going to do the things for which I exist and for which I was brought into the world? Or have I been made for this, to lie under the blankets and keep myself warm? But this is more pleasant. Do you exist then to take your pleasure, and not at all for action or exertion? Do you not see the little plants, the little birds, the ants, the spiders, the bees working together to put in order their separate parts of the universe? And are you unwilling to do the work of a human being, and do you not make haste to do that which is according to your nature? But it is necessary to take rest also. It is necessary: nature, however, has fixed bounds to this, too: she has fixed bounds both to eating and drinking, and yet you go beyond these bounds, beyond what is sufficient; yet in your acts it is not so, but you stop short of what you can do. So you do not love yourself, for if you did, you would love your nature and her will. But those who love their several arts exhaust themselves in working at them unwashed and without food; but you value your own nature less than the engraver values the engraving art, or the dancer the dancing art, or the lover of money values his money, or the vainglorious man his little glory. And such men, when they have an ardent passion for a thing, choose neither to eat nor to sleep rather than to perfect the things that they care for. But are the acts that concern society more vile in your eyes and less worthy of your labor?

2. How easy it is to repel and to wipe away every impression that is troublesome or unsuitable, and immediately to be in all tranquillity.

3. Judge every word and deed that are naturally fit for you, and do not be diverted by words of blame or criticism; if it is good to do or say something, do not consider it unworthy of yourself. For those persons have their peculiar leading principle and follow their peculiar movement; ignore them and go straight on, following your own nature and the common nature; and the way of both is one.

4. I go through the things that happen according to nature until I shall

fall and rest, breathing out my last breath into that element out of which I daily draw it in, and falling upon the earth out of which my father collected the seed, and my mother the blood, and my nurse the milk; out of which during so many years I have been supplied with food and drink; which bears me when I tread on it and abuse it for so many purposes.

5. You say, "Men cannot admire me for the sharpness of my wits." So be it: but there are many other things of which you cannot say, "I am not formed for them by nature." Show those qualities then that are altogether in your power: sincerity, gravity, endurance of labor, aversion to pleasure, contentment with your portion and with a simple life, benevolence, frankness, no love of superfluity, freedom from trifling magnanimity. Do you see how many qualities you are immediately able to exhibit, in which there is no excuse of natural incapacity and unfitness, and yet you still remain voluntarily below the mark? Or are you compelled through being defectively furnished by nature to grumble, and to be stingy, and to flatter, and to find fault with your poor body, and to try to please men, and to make great display, and to be so restless in your mind? No, by the gods: but you might have been delivered from these things long ago. Only if in truth you can be charged with being rather slow and dull of comprehension, you must exert yourself about this also, not neglecting it nor yet taking pleasure in your dullness.

6. One man, when he has done a service to another, is ready to set it down to his account as a favor conferred. Another is not ready to do this, but still thinks of the man as his debtor, and he knows what he has done. A third in a manner does not even know what he has done, but he is like a vine that has produced grapes and seeks for nothing more after it has once produced its proper fruit. As a horse when he has run, a dog when he has tracked the game, a bee when it has made the honey, so a man when he has done a good act, does not call out for others to come and see, but he goes on to another act, as a vine goes on to produce again the grapes in season. Must a man then be one of these, who in a manner act thus without observing it? Yes. But this very thing is necessary, the observation of what a man is doing: for, it may be said, it is characteristic of the social animal to perceive that he is working in a social manner and, indeed, to wish that his social partner also should perceive it. It is true what you say, but you do not rightly understand what is now said: and for this reason you will become one of those of whom I spoke before, for even they are misled by a certain show of reason. But if you will choose to understand the meaning of what is said, do not fear that for this reason you will omit any social act.

7. A prayer of the Athenians: Rain, rain, O dear Zeus, down on the

ploughed fields of the Athenians and on the plains. In truth we ought
not to pray at all, or we ought to pray in this simple and noble fashion.

8. Just as we must understand when it is said that Aesculapius prescribed to this man horse-exercise or bathing in cold water or going
without shoes; so we must understand it when it is said that the nature
of the universe prescribed to this man disease or mutilation or loss or
anything else of the kind. For in the first case "prescribed" means something like this: he prescribed this for this man as a thing adapted to procure health; and in the second case it means: that which happens to
(or, suits) every man is fixed in a manner for him suitable to his destiny. For this is what we mean when we say that things are suitable to
us, as the workmen say of squared stones in walls or the pyramids, that
they are suitable, when they fit in some kind of connection. For there
is altogether one fitness, harmony. And as the universe is made up out
of all bodies to be the body it is, so out of all existing causes necessity
(destiny) is made up to be the cause it is. And even those who are completely ignorant understand what I mean, for they say, It (necessity, destiny) brought this to such a person. This then was brought and this was
prescribed to him. Let us then receive these things, as well as those that
Aesculapius prescribes. As a matter of course, many, even among his
prescriptions, are disagreeable, but we accept them in the hope of
health. Let the perfecting and accomplishment of the things, which
the common nature judges to be good, be judged by you to be of the
same kind as your health. And so accept everything that happens, even
if it seems disagreeable, because it leads to this, to the health of the universe and to the prosperity and felicity of Zeus (the universe). For he
would not have brought on any man what he has brought if it were not
useful for the whole. Neither does the nature of anything, whatever it
may be, cause anything that is not suitable to that which is directed by
it. For two reasons then it is right to be content with what happens to
you; the one, because it was done for you and prescribed for you, and
in a manner had reference to you, originally from the most ancient
causes spun with your destiny; and the other, because even what comes
separately to every man is to the power that administers the universe a
cause of felicity and perfection, even of its very continuance. For the
integrity of the whole is mutilated if you cut off anything whatever from
the conjunction and the continuity either of the parts or of the causes.
And you do cut off, as far as it is in your power, when you are dissatisfied, and in a manner try to put anything out of the way.

9. Do not be disgusted, discouraged, or dissatisfied if you do not suc-
ceed in doing everything according to right principles; but when you

have failed, return again, and be content if the greater part of what you do is consistent with man's nature, and love this to which you return; and do not return to philosophy as if she were a master, but act like those who have sore eyes and apply a bit of sponge and egg, or as another applies a plaster or drenching with water. For thus you will not fail to obey reason, and you will repose in it. And remember that philosophy requires only the things that your nature requires; but you would have something else that is not according to nature. It may be objected, "What is more agreeable than what I am doing?" But is not this the very reason why pleasure deceives us? And consider if magnanimity, freedom, simplicity, equanimity, and piety are not more agreeable. For what is more agreeable than wisdom itself, when you think of the security and the happy course of all things that depend on the faculty of understanding and knowledge?

10. Things are so shrouded that they have seemed to philosophers, not a few nor those common philosophers, altogether unintelligible; even to the Stoics themselves they seem difficult to understand. And all our assertions about these things are changeable; for where is the man who never changes? Turn your thoughts then to the objects themselves, and consider how short-lived they are and worthless, and that they may be in the possession of a catamite or a whore or a robber. Then turn to the morals of those who live with you, and it is hardly possible to endure even the most agreeable of them, to say nothing of a man being hardly able to endure himself. In such darkness then and dirt and in such constant flux both of substance and of time, and of motion and of things moved, what there is that is worth being highly prized or even an object of serious pursuit, I cannot imagine. But on the contrary it is a man's duty to comfort himself, and to wait for the natural dissolution and not to be vexed at the delay, but to rest in these principles only: the one, that nothing will happen to me which is not conformable to the nature of the universe; and the other, that it is in my power never to act contrary to my god and daimon: for there is no man who will compel me to this.

11. About what am I now employing my own soul? On every occasion I must ask myself this question, "What have I now in this part of me which they call the ruling principle? And whose soul have I now? That of a child, or of a young man, or of a feeble woman, or of a tyrant, or of a domestic animal, or of a wild beast?"

12. We may learn even from the kind of things that appear good to the many. For if any man should conceive certain things as being really good, such as prudence, temperance, justice, and fortitude, he

would not after having first conceived these endure to listen to anything that should not be in harmony with what is really good. But if a
man has first conceived as good the things that appear to the many to
be good, he will listen and readily receive as very applicable that which
was said by the comic writer. Thus even the many perceive the difference. For were it not so, this saying would not offend and would not be
rejected in the first case, while we receive it when it is said of wealth
and of the means that further luxury and fame. Go on then and ask if
we should value and think those things to be good, to which after their
first conception in the mind the words of the comic writer might be
aptly applied—that he who has them, through having them in such
abundance, has not a place in which to relieve himself.

13. I am composed of the formal and the material; and neither of
them will perish into nonexistence, as neither of them came into existence out of nonexistence. Every part of me then will be reduced by
change into some part of the universe, and that again will change into
another part of the universe, and so on forever. And by consequence of
such a change, I, too, exist, and those who begot me, and so on forever in the other direction. For nothing hinders us from saying so, even if
the universe is administered according to definite periods of revolution.

14. Reason and the reasoning art (philosophy) are powers that are
sufficient for themselves and for their own works. They move then from
a first principle that is their own, and they make their way to the end
that is proposed to them; and this is the reason why such acts are
named *catorthóseis*, or right acts, meaning that they proceed by the
right road.

15. None of these things ought to be called a man's that do not
belong to a man, as man. They are not required of a man, nor does
man's nature promise them, nor are they the means of man's nature
attaining its end. Neither then does the end of man lie in these things,
nor yet that which aids the accomplishment of this end, and that which
aids toward this end is that which is good. Besides, if any of these things
did belong to man, it would not be right for a man to despise them and
to set himself against them; nor would a man be worthy of praise who
showed that he did not want these things, nor would he who stinted
himself in any of them be good, if indeed these things were good. But
now the more of these things a man deprives himself of, or of other
things like them, or even when he is deprived of any of them, the more
patiently he endures the loss, just in the same degree he is a better man.

16. Such as are your habitual thoughts, such also will be the character of your mind; for the soul is dyed by the thoughts. Dye it then

with a continuous series of such thoughts as these: for instance, that where a man can live, there he can also live well. If he must live in a palace, then he can also live well in a palace. And again, consider that for whatever purpose each thing has been constituted, for this it has been constituted, and toward this it is carried; and its end is in that toward which it is carried; and where the end is, there also is the advantage and the good of each thing. Now the good for the reasonable animal is society; for that we are made for society has been shown above. Is it not plain that the inferior exist for the sake of the superior? But the things that have life are superior to those that do not, and of those that have life, the superior are those that have reason.

17. To seek what is impossible is madness: and it is impossible that the bad should not do.something of this kind.

18. Nothing happens to any man that he is not formed by nature to bear. The same things happen to another, and either because he does not see that they have happened or because he would show a great spirit, he is firm and remains unharmed. It is a shame then that ignorance and conceit should be stronger than wisdom.

19. Things themselves cannot touch the soul, not in the least degree; nor have they admission to the soul, nor can they turn or move the soul: the soul turns and moves itself alone, and whatever judgments it may think proper to make, such it makes by remaking for itself the things that present themselves to it.

20. In one respect man is the nearest thing to me, so far as I must do good to men and endure them. But so far as some men make themselves obstacles to my proper acts, man becomes to me one of the things that are indifferent, no less than the sun or wind or a wild beast. Now it is true that these may impede my action, but they are no impediments to my affects and disposition, which have the power of acting conditionally and changing: for the mind converts and changes every hindrance to its activity into an aid; and so that which is a hindrance is made a furtherance to an act, and an obstacle on the road helps us along this road.

21. Revere that which is best in the universe; and this is that which makes use of all things and directs all things. And in like manner also revere that which is best in yourself; and this is of the same kind as that. For in yourself also, that which makes use of everything else, is this, and your life is directed by this.

22. That which does no harm to the state does no harm to the citizen. In the case of every appearance of harm, apply this rule: if the state is not harmed by this, neither am I harmed. But if the state is harmed,

you must not be angry with him who does harm to the state. Show him where his error is.

23. Often think of the rapidity with which things pass by and disappear, both the things that are and the things that are produced. For substance is like a river in a continual flow, and the activities of things are in constant change, and the causes work in infinite varieties; and there is hardly anything that stands still. And consider what is near to you, this boundless abyss of the past and of the future in which all things disappear. How then is he not a fool who is puffed up with such things or plagued about them and makes himself miserable? For they vex him only for a time, and a short time.

24. Think of the universal substance, of which you have a very small portion; and of universal time, of which a short and indivisible interval has been assigned to you; and of that which is fixed by destiny, and how small a part of it you are.

25. Does another do me wrong? Let him look to it. He has his own disposition, his own activity. I now have what the universal nature wills me to have; and I do what my nature now wills me to do.

26. Let the part of your soul that leads and governs be undisturbed by the movements in the flesh, whether of pleasure or of pain; and let it not unite with them, but let it circumscribe itself and limit those affects to their parts. But when these affects rise up to the mind by virtue of that other sympathy that naturally exists in a body that is all one, then you must not strive to resist the sensation, for it is natural: but do not let the ruling part of itself add to the sensation the opinion that it is either good or bad.

27. Live with the gods. And he does live with the gods who constantly shows to them that his own soul is satisfied with its daimon, that portion of himself that Zeus has given to every man to be his guardian and guide, and that his soul does all that the daimon wishes. And this is every man's understanding and reason.

28. Are you angry with him whose armpits stink? Are you angry with him whose mouth smells foul? What good will this anger do you? He has such a mouth, he has such armpits: it is necessary that such an emanation must come from such things—but the man has reason, it will be said, and he is able, if he takes pains, to discover wherein he offends. Well then, and you, too, have reason: by your rational faculty stir up his rational faculty; show him his error, admonish him. For if he listens, you will cure him, and there is no need of anger, the stuff of tragic actors and whores.

29. As you intend to live when you are gone, so it is in your power to

live here. But if men do not permit you, then get away out of life, as if you were suffering no harm. The house is smoky, and I quit it. Why do you think that this is any trouble? But so long as nothing of the kind drives me out, I remain, am free, and no man shall hinder me from doing what I choose; and I choose to do what is according to the nature of the rational and social animal.

30. The intelligence of the universe is social. Accordingly it has made the inferior things for the sake of the superior, and it has fitted the superior to one another. You see how it has subordinated, coordinated, and assigned to everything its proper portion and has brought together into concord with one another the things that are the best.

31. How have you behaved hitherto to the gods, your parents, brethren, children, teachers, to those who looked after your infancy, to your friends, kinfolks, to your slaves? Consider if you have hitherto behaved to all in such a way that this way be said of you:

> Never has he wronged a man in deed or word.

And call to recollection both how many things you have passed through, and how many things you have been able to endure: and that the history of your life is now complete and your service is ended: and how many beautiful things you have seen: and how many pleasures and pains you have despised; and how many things called honorable you have spurned; and to how many ill-minded folks you have shown a kind disposition.

32. Why do unskilled and ignorant souls disturb him who has skill and knowledge? What soul then has skill and knowledge? That which knows beginning and end, and knows the reason that pervades all substance and through all time by fixed periods (revolutions) administers the universe.

33. Soon, very soon, you will be ashes or a skeleton, and either a name or not even a name; but name is sound and echo. And the things that are much valued in life are empty and rotten and trifling, and like little dogs biting one another, and little children quarrelling, laughing, and then straightaway weeping. But fidelity and modesty and justice and truth have fled "up to Olympus from the wide-spread earth." What then is there that still detains you here? The objects of sense are easily changed and never stand still, and the organs of perception are dull and easily receive false impressions; and the poor soul itself is an exhalation from blood. But to have good repute amidst such a world as this is an empty thing. Why then do you not wait in tranquillity for your

end, whether it is extinction or removal to another state? And until that time comes, what is sufficient? Why, what else than to venerate the gods and bless them, and to do good to men, and to practice tolerance and self-restraint; but as to everything that is beyond the limits of the poor flesh and breath, to remember that this is neither yours nor in your power.

34. You can pass your life in an equable flow of happiness if you can follow the right way and think and act in the right way. Two things are common both to the soul of God and to the soul of man, and to the soul of every rational being: not to be hindered by another; and to seek the good in the disposition to justice and the practice of it, and in this to let your desire find its termination.

35. If this is neither my own badness, nor an effect of my own badness, and the common weal is not injured, why am I troubled about it? And what is the harm to the common weal?

36. Do not be carried along inconsiderately by the appearance of things, but give help to all according to your ability and their fitness; and if they should have sustained loss in matters that are indifferent, do not imagine this to be a damage. For it is a bad habit. Emulate the old man who, when he went away, asked for his foster-child's top, knowing that it was only a top.

When you are haranguing the populace, have you forgotten, man, what these things really mean? Yes; but they are objects of great concern to these people. Will you, too, then be made a fool for these things? "I was once a fortunate man, but I lost it, I know not how." But "fortunate" means that a man has assigned to himself a good fortune: and a good fortune is good disposition of the soul, good emotions, good actions.

BOOK VI

The substance of the universe is obedient and compliant; and the reason that governs it has in itself no cause for doing evil, for it has no malice, nor does it do evil to anything, nor is anything harmed by it. But all things are made and perfected according to this reason.

2. Let it make no difference to you whether you are cold or warm, if you are doing your duty; and whether you are drowsy or satisfied with sleep; and whether ill-spoken of or praised; and whether dying or doing something else. For it is one of the acts of life, this act by which we die: it is sufficient then in this act also to do well what we have in hand.

3. Look within. Let neither the peculiar quality of anything nor its value escape you.

4. All existing things soon change, and they will either be reduced to vapor, if indeed all substance is one, or they will be dispersed.

5. The reason that governs knows what its own disposition is, and what it does, and on what material it works.

6. The best way of avenging yourself is not to become like the wrongdoer.

7. Take pleasure in one thing and rest in it: in passing from one social act to another social act, thinking of God.

8. The ruling principle is that which rouses and turns itself and while it makes itself such as it is and such as it wills to be, it also makes everything that happens appear to itself to be such as it wills.

9. Every single thing is accomplished in conformity to the nature of the universe, for certainly it is not in conformity to any other nature that each thing is accomplished, either a nature that comprehends this nature externally or a nature that is comprehended within this nature or a nature independent of this nature and external to it.

10. The universe is either a confusion, a mutual involution of things and a dispersion; or it is unity and order and providence. If then it is the former, why do I desire to tarry in a fortuitous combination of things and such a disorder? And why do I care about anything else than how I shall at last become earth? And why am I disturbed, for the dispersion

of my elements will happen whatever I do. But if the other supposition is true, I venerate, and I am firm, and I trust in him who governs.

11. When you have been compelled by circumstances to be disturbed in a manner, quickly return to yourself and do not continue out of tune longer than the compulsion lasts; for you will have more mastery over the harmony by continually recurring to it.

12. If you had a stepmother and a mother at the same time, you would be dutiful to your stepmother, but still you would constantly return to your mother. Let the court and philosophy now be stepmother and mother to you: return to philosophy frequently and repose in her, through whom what you meet with in the court appears tolerable to you, and you appear tolerable in the court.

13. When we have meat before us and such eatables, we receive the impression that this is the dead body of a fish, and this is the dead body of a bird or of a pig; and again, that this Falernian is only a little grape juice, and this purple robe some sheep's wool dyed with the blood of a shellfish; or, in the matter of sexual intercourse, that it is merely an internal attrition and the spasmodic expulsion of semen: such then are these impressions, and they reach the things themselves and penetrate them, and so we see the things as they truly are. Just in the same way ought we to act all through life, and where there are things that appear most worthy of our approbation, we ought to lay them bare and look at their worthlessness and strip them of all the words by which they are exalted. For outward show is a wonderful perverter of reason, and when you are most sure that you are employed about things worth your pains, it is then that it cheats you most. Consider then what Crates says of Xenocrates himself.

14. Most of the things that the multitude admire may be classed as objects of the most general kind, those that are held together by cohesion or natural organization, such as stones, fig trees, vines, olives. But those that are admired by men who are a little more reasonable may be classed as things that are held together by a living principle, as flocks, herds. Those that are admired by men who are still more instructed are the things held together by a rational soul, not however a universal soul, but rational so far as it is a soul skilled in some art, or expert in some other way, or simply rational so far as it possesses a number of slaves. But he who values a rational soul, a soul universal and fitted for political life, regards nothing else except this; and above all things he keeps his soul in a condition and in an activity conformable to reason and social life, and he cooperates to this end with those who are of the same kind as himself.

15. Some things are hurrying into existence, and others are hurrying out of it; and of that which is coming into existence, part is already extinguished. Motions and changes are continually renewing the world, just as the uninterrupted course of time is always renewing the infinite duration of ages. In this flowing stream, then, on which there is no abiding, what is there of the things that hurry by on which a man would set a high price? It would be just as if a man should fall in love with one of the sparrows that fly by, when has already passed out of sight. Something of this kind is the very life of every man, like the exhalation of the blood and the respiration of the air. For such as it is to have once drawn in the air and to have given it back, which we do every moment, just the same is it with the whole respiratory power, which you received at birth yesterday and the day before, to give it back to the element from which you first drew it.

16. Neither is transpiration, as in plants, a thing to be valued, nor respiration, as in domesticated animals and wild beasts, nor the receiving of impressions by the appearances of things, nor being moved by the desires as puppets by strings, nor assembling in herds, nor being nourished by food; for this is just like the act of separating and parting with the useless part of our food. What then is worth being valued? To be received with clapping of hands? No. Neither must we value the clapping of tongues, for the praise that comes from the many is a clapping of tongues. Suppose then that you have given up this worthless thing called fame, what remains that is worth valuing? This, in my opinion: to move yourself and to restrain yourself in conformity to your proper constitution, to which end all employments and arts lead. For every art aims at this, that the thing that has been made should be adapted to the work for which it has been made; and the vine planter who looks after the vine, the horsebreaker, and he who trains the dog seek this end. And the education and the teaching of youth aim at the same thing. In this then is the value of the education and the teaching. And if this is well, you will not seek anything else. Will you not cease to value many other things, too? Then you will be neither free, nor sufficient for your own happiness, nor without passion. For of necessity you must be envious, jealous, and suspicious of those who can take away those things, and plot against those who have that which is valued by you. Of necessity a man must be altogether in a state of perturbation who wants any of these things; and besides, he must often find fault with the gods. But to revere and honor your own mind will make you content with yourself, in harmony with society, and in agreement with the gods, praising all that they give and have ordered.

17. Above, below, all around are the movements of the elements. But the motion of virtue is in none of these: it is something more divine and, advancing by a way hardly observed, it goes happily on its road.

18. How strangely men act. They will not praise those who are living at the same time and living with themselves; but to be themselves praised by posterity, by those whom they have never seen or ever will see, this they set much value on. But this is very much the same as if you should be grieved because those who have lived before you did not praise you.

19. If it is difficult to accomplish something by yourself, do not think that it is impossible for man: but if anything is possible for man and conformable to his nature, think that this can be attained by you, too.

20. In the gymnastic exercises suppose that a man has torn you with his nails, and by dashing against your head has inflicted a wound. Well, we neither show any signs of vexation, nor are we offended, nor do we suspect him afterward as a treacherous fellow; and yet we are on our guard against him, not, however, as an enemy, nor yet with suspicion, but we quietly get out of his way. Emulate this behavior in all the other parts of life; let us overlook many things in those who are like antagonists in the gymnasium. For it is in our power, as I said, to get out of the way and to have no suspicion or hatred.

21. If any man is able to convince me and show me that I do not think or act right, I will gladly change; for I seek the truth by which no man was ever injured. But he is injured who abides in his error and ignorance.

22. I do my duty: other things do not trouble me; for they are either things without life, or things without reason, or things that have rambled and do not know the way.

23. As to the animals that have no reason and generally all things and objects, since you have reason and they have none, make use of them with a generous and liberal spirit. But toward human beings, since they have reason, behave in a social spirit. And on all occasions call on the gods, and do not perplex yourself about the length of time in which you shall do this; for even three hours so spent are sufficient.

24. Alexander the Macedonian and his groom were brought to the same state by death; for either they were received among the same seminal principles of the universe, or they were alike dispersed among the atoms.

25. Consider how many things in the same indivisible time take place in each of us, things that concern the body and things that con-

cern the soul: and so you will not wonder if many more things, or rather all things that arise in the unity we call Cosmos, exist in it at the same time.

26. If any man should ask you how the name Antoninus is written, would you, with a straining of the voice, utter each letter? What if the questioner grew angry, would you be angry, too? Would you not go on with composure and spell out every letter? Just so then in this life also remember that every duty is made up of certain parts. These it is your duty to observe and to go on your way and finish that which is set before you without being disturbed or showing anger toward those who are angry with you.

27. How cruel it is not to allow men to strive after the things that appear to them to be suitable to their nature and profitable! And yet in a manner you allow them to do this when you are vexed because they do wrong. For they are certainly moved toward things because they suppose them to be suitable to their nature and profitable to them. "But it is not so." Teach them then, and show them without being angry.

28. Death is a cessation of the impressions through the senses, and of the pulling of the strings that move the appetites, and of the discursive movements of the thoughts, and of the service to the flesh.

29. It is a shame for the soul to be first to give way in this life, when your body does not give way.

30. Take care that you are not made into a Caesar, that you are not dyed with this dye; for such things happen. Keep yourself then simple, good, pure, serious, free from affectation, a friend of justice, a worshipper of the gods, kind, affectionate, strenuous in all proper acts. Strive to continue to be such as philosophy wished to make you. Revere the gods, and help men. Life is short. There is only one fruit of this earthly life, a pious disposition and social acts. Do everything as a disciple of Antoninus. Remember his constancy in every act that was conformable to reason, and his evenness in all things, and his piety, and the serenity of his countenance, and his sweetness, and his disregard of empty fame, and his efforts to understand things; and how he would never let anything pass without having first most carefully examined it and clearly understood it; and how he bore with those who blamed him unjustly without blaming them in return; how he did nothing in a hurry; and how he refused to listen to calumnies, and how exact an examiner of manners and actions he was; and not given to reproach people, nor timid, nor suspicious, nor a sophist; and with how little he was satisfied, such as lodging, bed, dress, food, servants; and how labo-

rious and patient; and how he was able on account of his sparing diet to hold out to the evening, not even requiring to relieve himself by any evacuations except at the usual hour; and his firmness and uniformity in his friendships; and how he tolerated freedom of speech in those who opposed his opinions; and the pleasure that he had when any man showed him anything better; and how religious he was without superstition. Imitate all this that you may have as good a conscience, when your last hour comes, as he had.

31. Return to your sober senses and call yourself back; and when you have roused yourself from sleep and have perceived that they were only dreams that troubled you, now in your waking hours look at these (the things about you) as you did look at those (the dreams).

32. I consist of a little body and a soul. Now to this little body all things are indifferent, for it is not able to perceive differences. But to the understanding only those things are indifferent that are not the works of its own activity. But whatever things are the works of its own activity, all these are in its power—and of these, however, only those that are done with reference to the present; for as to the future and the past activities of the mind, even these are indifferent for the present.

33. Neither the labor of the hand nor that of the foot is contrary to nature so long as the foot does the foot's work and the hand the hand's. So then neither to a man as a man is his labor contrary to nature as long as it does the things of a man. But if the labor is not contrary to his nature, neither is it an evil to him.

34. How many pleasures have been enjoyed by robbers, patricides, tyrants.

35. Do you not see how the handicraftsmen accommodate themselves up to a certain point to those who are not skilled in their craft—nevertheless they cling to the reason (the principles) of their art and brook no departure from it? Is it not strange if the architect and the physician shall have more respect for the reason (the principles) of their own arts than man has for his own reason, which is common to him and the gods?

36. Asia and Europe are corners of the universe: all the sea a drop in the universe; Athos a little clod of the universe: all the present time is a point in eternity. All things are little, changeable, perishable. All things come from that universal ruling power either directly or mediately. And accordingly the lion's gaping jaws, and that which is poisonous, and every harmful thing, such as a thorn or mud, are byproducts of the grand and beautiful. Do not then imagine that they are of anoth-

er kind from that which you venerate, but form a just opinion of the source of all.

37. He who has seen present things has seen all, both everything that has taken place from all eternity and everything that will be for time without end; for all things are of one kin and of one form.

38. Frequently consider the connection of all things in the universe and their relation to one another. For in a manner all things are implicated with one another, and all in this way are friendly to one another; for one thing comes in order after another, and this is by virtue of the active movement and mutual conspiration and the unity of the substance.

39. Adapt yourself to the things with which your lot has been cast: and the men among whom you have received your portion, love them, but do it truly, sincerely.

40. Every instrument, tool, vessel, if it does that for which it has been made, is good, and yet he who made it is not there. But in the things that are held together by nature, there abides in them the power that made them; wherefore the more is it fit to revere this power and to think that if you live and act according to its will, everything in you is in conformity to intelligence. And thus also in the universe the things that belong to it are in conformity to intelligence.

41. If you suppose that the things that are not within your power are good or bad for you, then if you suffer a bad thing or the loss of a good thing, you will blame the gods and hate men, too: those who are the cause of the misfortune or the loss, or those who are suspected of being the likely cause; and indeed we do a great injustice when we dwell on such matters. But if we judge only those things that are in our power to be good or bad, there remains no reason either for finding fault with God or standing in a hostile attitude to man.

42. We are all working together to one end, some with knowledge and design, and others without knowing what they do; like sleeping men, who are, according to Heraclitus, laborers and cooperators in the things that take place in the universe. But men cooperate in different ways: and even those cooperate abundantly who find fault with what happens and try to oppose and hinder it; for the universe had need even of such men as these. It remains then for you to understand among what kind of workmen you place yourself; for he who rules all things will certainly make right use of you, and he will receive you among some part of the cooperators and of those whose labors conduce to one end. But do not play the kind of mean and ridiculous part that Chrysippus speaks of in his play.

43. Does the sun undertake to do the work of the rain, or

Aesculapius the work of the fruit-bearer (the earth)? Isn't each star different yet working with the others toward the same end?

44. If the gods have deliberated about me and about the things that must happen to me, they have determined well, for it is not easy to imagine a deity deprived of forethought; and as to doing me harm, why should they have any desire toward that? For what advantage would result to them from this or to the whole, which is the special object of their providence? But if they have not determined about me individually, they have certainly determined about the whole at least, and I ought to accept with pleasure and be content with the things that happen by way of sequence in this general arrangement. But if the gods deliberate about nothing—which it is wicked to believe, or if we do believe it, let us neither sacrifice nor pray nor swear by them nor do anything else that we do as if the gods were present and lived with us—but if, however, the gods deliberate about none of the things that concern us, I am able to deliberate about myself, and I can inquire about what is useful; and what is useful to every man is that which is conformable to his own constitution and nature. But my nature is rational and social; and my city and country, so far as I am Antoninus, is Rome; but so far as I am a man, it is the world. The things then that are useful to these cities are alone useful to me.

45. Whatever happens to every man accrues to the interest of the universal: this might be sufficient. But further you will observe this general truth, that whatever is profitable to any man is profitable also to other men. But let the word *profitable* be taken here in the common sense as said of things of the middle kind, neither good nor bad.

46. You might observe in the amphitheater and such places that the continual sight of the same things and the uniformity make the spectacle wearisome; so it is in the whole of life: for all things above, below, are the same and from the same. How long then?

47. Think continually that all kinds of men, pursuits, and nations are dead, so that your thoughts come down even to Philistion and Phoebus and Origanion. Now turn your thoughts to the other kinds of men. To that place then we must remove, where there are so many great orators, and so many noble philosophers, Heraclitus, Pythagoras, Socrates; so many heroes of former days, and so many generals after them, and tyrants; besides these, Eudoxus, Hipparchus, Archimedes, and other men of acute natural talents, great minds, lovers of labor, versatile, confident, mockers even of the perishable and ephemeral life of man, as Menippus and such as are like him. Consider that all these have long been in the dust. What harm then is this to them; and what to those

whose names are altogether unknown? One thing here is worth a great deal: to pass your life in truth and justice, with a benevolent disposition even to liars and unjust men.

48. When you wish to delight yourself, think of the virtues of those who live with you; for instance, the activity of one, the modesty of another, the liberality of a third, and some other good quality of a fourth. For nothing delights so much as the examples of the virtues when they are exhibited in the morals of those who live with us and present themselves in abundance, as far as is possible. Hence we must keep them before us.

49. You are not dissatisfied, I suppose, because you weigh only so many pounds and not three hundred. Do not be dissatisfied then that you must live only so many years and not more; for as you are satisfied with the amount of substance that has been assigned to you, so be content with the time.

50. Let us try to persuade men. But act even against their will when the principles of justice lead that way. If, however, any man by using force stands in your way, have recourse to contentment and tranquillity, employing this hindrance as a spur to the exercise of some other virtue; and remember that thy attempt was limited, that you did not desire to do impossibilities. What then did you desire? Some such effort as this. But you attain your object if the things to which you were moved are accomplished.

51. He who loves fame considers another man's activity to be his own good; and he who loves pleasure, his own sensations; but he who has understanding considers his own acts to be his own good.

52. It is in our power to have no opinion about a thing and not to be disturbed in our soul; for things themselves have no natural power to form our judgments.

53. Accustom yourself to attend carefully to what is said by another, and as much as it is possible, try to inhabit the speaker's mind.

54. That which is not good for the swarm is not good for the bee either.

55. If sailors abused the helmsman or the sick the doctor, would they listen to anybody else? How could the helmsman secure the safety of those in the ship or the doctor the health of those whom he attends?

56. How many together with whom I came into the world are already gone out of it!

57. To the jaundiced honey tastes bitter, and to those bitten by mad dogs water causes fear; and to little children the ball is a fine thing. Why then am I angry? Do you think that a false opinion has less power

than the bile in the jaundiced or the poison in someone bitten by a mad dog?

58. No man will hinder you from living according to the reason of your own nature: nothing will happen to you contrary to the reason of the universal nature.

59. What kind of people are those whom men wish to please, and for what objects, and by what kind of acts? How soon will time cover all things, and how many it has covered already.

BOOK VII

What is badness? It is that which you have often seen. Amidst all that happens, keep in mind that you have seen it often. Everywhere up and down you will find the same things, with which the old histories are filled, those of the middle period and those of our own day; with which cities and houses are filled now. There is nothing new: all things are both familiar and short-lived.

2. How can our principles become dead unless the impressions (thoughts) that correspond to them are extinguished? But it is in your power continuously to fan these thoughts into a flame. I can form the opinion that I ought to have about anything. If I am able to do so, why am I disturbed? The things that are external to my mind have no relation at all to my mind. Let this be the state of your affects, and you will stand erect. To recover your life is in your power. Look at things again as you used to look at them; for in this consists the recovery of your life.

3. The idle business of show, plays on the stage, flocks of sheep, herds, exercises with spears, a bone cast to little dogs, a bit of bread into fish ponds, laborings of ants and burden carrying, runnings about of frightened little mice, puppets pulled by strings—all alike. It is your duty then in the midst of such things to show good humor and not a proud air; to understand, however, that every man is worth just so much as the things about which he busies himself.

4. In discourse you must attend to what is said, and in every action you must observe what is being done. And in the latter you should see immediately what end is intended, but in the former watch carefully what thing is signified.

5. Is my understanding sufficient for this or not? If it is sufficient, I use it for the work as an instrument given by universal nature. But if it is not sufficient, then either I retire from the work and give way to him who is able to do it better—unless there be some reason why I ought not to do so—or I do it as well as I can, taking to help me the man who, with the aid of my ruling principle, can do what is now fit and useful for the general good. For in whatever I do, either by myself or with

47

another, I must direct my energies to this alone, that it shall conduce to the common interest and be in harmony with it.

6. How many, after being celebrated by fame, have been given up to oblivion; and how many who have celebrated the fame of others have long been dead.

7. Do not be ashamed to be helped; for it is your business to do your duty like a soldier in the assault on a town. What if, being lame, you cannot mount up on the battlements alone, but with the help of another it is possible?

8. Do not let the future disturb you, for you will arrive there, if you arrive, with the same reason you now apply to the present.

9. All things are mutually intertwined, and the bond is holy; and there is hardly anything unconnected with any other thing. For things have been coordinated, and they combine to form one universal order. For there is one universe made up of all things, and one God who pervades all things, and one substance, and one law, one common reason in all intelligent animals, and one truth; if indeed there is also one perfection for all animals that are of the same stock and participate in the same reason.

10. Everything material soon disappears in the substance of the whole; and everything formal (causal) is very soon taken back into the universal reason; and the memory of everything is very soon overwhelmed in time.

11. To the rational animal the same act is at once according to nature and according to reason.

12. Be upright, or be made upright.

13. The principle that obtains where limbs and body unite to form one organism, holds good also for rational things with their separate individualities, constituted as they are to work in conjunction. And the perception of this will be more apparent to you, if you often say to yourself that you am a member ($\mu\epsilon\lambda o\sigma$) of the system of rational beings. But if (using the letter r) you say that you are a part ($\mu\epsilon\rho o\sigma$), you do not yet love men from your heart; beneficence does not delight you for its own sake; you still do it barely as a thing of propriety and not yet as doing good to yourself.

14. Let there fall externally what will on whatever can feel the effects of this fall. For that which feels will complain, if it so chooses. But I, unless I think that what has happened is an evil, am not injured. And it is in my power not to think so.

15. Whatever any one does or says, I must be good, just as if the emerald (or the gold or the purple) were always saying "Whatever any one does or says, I must be emerald and keep my color."

16. The ruling faculty does not disturb itself; I mean, does not frighten itself or stir up its desires. But if anyone else can frighten or disturb it, let him do so. For the faculty itself will not by its own assumptions turn itself into such ways. Let the body itself take care, if it can, that it suffer nothing, and let it speak, if it suffers. But the soul itself, that which is subject to fear, to pain, which has completely the power of forming a judgment about these things, will suffer nothing, for it will never deviate into such a judgment. The leading principle in itself wants nothing, unless it creates its own needs; and therefore it is both free from perturbation and unimpeded if it does not disturb and impede itself.

17. Eudaimonia (happiness) is a good daimon, or a good thing. What then are you doing here, O imagination? Go back to wherever you came from, I entreat you by the gods, for I do not want you. But you have come according to your old fashion. I am not angry with you: go away.

18. Is any man afraid of change? What can take place without change? What then is more pleasing or more suitable to the universal nature? And can you take a hot bath unless the wood for the fire undergoes a change? And can you be nourished unless the food undergoes a change? And can anything else that is useful be accomplished without change? Do you not see then that for yourself also to change is just the same, and equally necessary for the universal nature?

19. Through the universal substance as through a furious torrent all bodies are carried, being by their nature united with and cooperating with the whole, as the parts of our body with one another. How many a Chrysippus, how many a Socrates, how many an Epictetus has time already swallowed up? And let the same thought occur to you with reference to every man and thing.

20. Only one thing troubles me, lest I should do something that the constitution of man does not allow, or in a way it does not allow, or what it does not allow now.

21. In a little while you will have forgotten everything; in a little while everything will have forgotten you.

22. It is peculiar to man to love even those who do wrong. And this happens, if when they do wrong it occurs to you that they are fellow humans and that they do wrong through ignorance and unintentionally, and that soon both of you will die; and above all, that the wrongdoer has done you no harm, for he has not made your ruling faculty worse than it was before.

23. The universal nature out of the universal substance, as if it were wax, now molds a horse, and when it has broken this up, it uses the

material for a tree, then for a man, then for something else; and each of these things subsists for a very short time. But it is no hardship for the vessel to be broken up, just as there was none in its being fastened together.

24. A scowling look is altogether unnatural; when it is often assumed, the result is that all comeliness dies away, and at last is so completely extinguished that it cannot be again lighted up at all. Try to conclude from this very fact that it is contrary to reason. For if even the perception of doing wrong departs, what reason is there for living any longer?

25. Nature, which governs the whole, will soon change all things that you see, and out of their substance will make other things, and again other things from the substance of them, in order that the world may be ever new.

26. When a man has done you wrong, immediately consider with what opinion about good or evil he has done wrong. For when you have seen this, you will pity him, and will neither wonder nor be angry. For either you yourself think the same thing to be good that he does or another thing of the same kind. It is your duty then to pardon him. But if you do not think such things to be good or evil, you will more readily be well disposed to him who is in error.

27. Think not so much of what you lack as of what you have: but of the things that you have, select the best, and then reflect how eagerly you would have sought them if you did not have them. At the same time, however, take care that you do not through being so pleased with them accustom yourself to overvalue them, so as to be disturbed if you should ever not have them.

28. Retire into yourself. It is characteristic of the rational ruling faculty to be satisfied with its own righteous dealing and the peace which that brings.

29. Wipe out the imagination. Stop the pulling of the strings. Confine yourself to the present. Understand well what happens either to you or to another. Divide and distribute every object into the causal (formal) and the material. Think of your last hour. Let the wrong that is done by a man stay there where the wrong was done.

30. Direct your attention to what is said. Let your understanding enter into the things that are done and the things that are doing them.

31. Adorn yourself with simplicity and modesty and with indifference toward the things that lie between virtue and vice. Love mankind. Follow God. The poet says that law rules all, but in truth there are only elements. And it is enough to remember that law rules all.

32. About death: Whether it is a dispersion, or a resolution into atoms, or annihilation, it is either extinction or change.

33. About pain: The pain that is intolerable carries us off; but that which lasts a long time is tolerable; and the mind maintains its own tranquillity by retiring into itself, and the ruling faculty is not made worse. But the parts that are harmed by pain, let them, if they can, give their opinion about it.

34. About fame: Look at the minds of those who seek fame, observe what they are, and what kind of things they avoid, and what kind of things they pursue. And consider that as the heaps of sand piled on one another hide the former sands, so in life the events that go before are soon covered by those that come after.

35. From Plato: "'The man who has an elevated mind and takes a view of all time and of all substance, do you suppose it possible for him to think that human life is anything great?' 'It is not possible,' he said. 'Such a man then will think that death also is no evil.' 'Certainly not.'"

36. From Antisthenes: "It is royal to do good and to be abused."

37. It is a base thing for the countenance to be obedient and to regulate and compose itself as the mind commands, and for the mind not to be regulated and composed by itself.

38. It is not right to vex ourselves at things,
    For they care nought about it,

39. To the immortal gods and us give joy.

40. Life must be reaped like the ripe ears of corn:
    One man is born; another dies.

41. If gods care not for me and for my children,
    There is a reason for it.

42. For the good is with me, and the just.

43. No joining others in their wailing, no violent emotion.

44. From Plato: "I would make this man a sufficient answer, which is this: You are mistaken if you think that a man who is good for anything at all ought to consider the risks of life or death, but rather should consider only in all that he does, whether he is doing what is just or unjust, and the works of a good or a bad man.

45. For thus it is, men of Athens, in truth: wherever a man has placed himself, thinking it the best place for him, or has been placed by a commander, there in my opinion he ought to stay and to abide the hazard, taking nothing into the reckoning, either death or anything else, before the baseness of deserting his post.

46. But, my good friend, reflect whether that which is noble and good is not something different from saving and being saved; for as to a

man living such or such a time, at least one who is really a man, consider if this is not a thing to be dismissed from the thoughts: and there must be no love of life: but as to these matters a man must entrust them to the deity and believe what the women say, that no man can escape his destiny, the next inquiry being how he may best live the time that he has to live."

47. Look round at the courses of the stars, as if you were going along with them; and constantly consider the changes of the elements into one another; for such thoughts purge away the filth of our earthly life.

48. This a fine saying of Plato: That he who is discoursing about men should look also at earthly things as if he viewed them from some higher place; should look at them in their assemblies, armies, agricultural labors, marriages, treaties, births, deaths, noise of the courts of justice, desert places, various nations of barbarians, feasts, lamentations, markets, a mixture of all things and an orderly combination of contraries.

49. Consider the past; such great changes of political supremacies. You may foresee also the things that will be. For they will certainly be of like form, and it is not possible that they should deviate from the order of the things that take place now: accordingly to have contemplated human life for forty years is the same as to have contemplated it for ten thousand years. For what more will you see?

50. All that has grown from the earth returns to the earth,
      But that which has sprung from heavenly seed,
      Back to the heavenly realms returns.

This is either a dissolution of the closely linked atoms, or a similar dispersion of the nonsentient elements.

51. With food and drinks and cunning magic arts
      Turning the channel's course to 'scape from death.
              The breeze that heaven has sent
      We must endure, and toil without complaining.

52. Another may be more expert in casting his opponent; but he is not more social, nor more modest, nor better disciplined to meet all that happens, nor more considerate with respect to the faults of his neighbors.

53. Where any work can be done conformably to the reason that is common to gods and men, there we have nothing to fear: for where we are able to get profit by means of a successful activity and proceeds according to our constitution, there no harm is to be suspected.

54. Everywhere and at all times it is in your power piously to acqui-

esce in your present condition, and to behave justly to those around you, and to exert your skill upon your present thoughts, that nothing shall steal into them without being well examined.

55. Do not look around you to discover other men's ruling principles, but look straight to this, to what nature leads you, both universal nature through the things that happen to you, and your own nature through the acts you must perform. But every being ought to do that which is according to its constitution; and all other things have been constituted for the sake of rational beings, just as among irrational things the inferior for the sake of the superior, but the rational for the sake of one another.

The prime principle then in man's constitution is the social. And the second is not to yield to the persuasions of the body, for it is the peculiar office of the rational and intelligent motion to circumscribe itself, and never to be overpowered either by the motion of the senses or of the appetites, for both are animal; but the intelligent motion claims superiority and does not permit itself to be overpowered by the others. And with good reason, for it is formed by nature to use all of them. The third thing in the rational constitution is freedom from error and from deception. Let then the ruling principle, holding fast to these things, go straight on, and it has what is its own.

56. Consider yourself to be dead, and to have completed your life up to the present time; and live, according to nature, the remainder that is allowed you.

57. Love only that which happens to you and is spun with the thread of your destiny. For what is more suitable?

58. In everything that happens, keep before your eyes those to whom the same things happened, and how they were vexed, and treated them as strange things, and found fault with them: and now where are they? Nowhere. Why then do you, too, choose to act in the same way? And why do you not leave these agitations, which are foreign to nature, to those who cause them and those who are moved by them? And why are you not altogether intent upon the right way of making use of the things that happen to you? For then you will use them well, and they will be a material for you to work on. Only attend to yourself, and resolve to be a good man in every act that you do: and remember . . .

59. Look within. Within is the fountain of good, and it will ever bubble up, if you will ever dig.

60. The body ought to be compact, and to show no irregularity either in motion or attitude. For what the mind shows in the face by main-

taining in it the expression of intelligence and propriety, that ought to be required also in the whole body. But all of these things should be observed without affectation.

61. The art of life is more like the wrestler's art than the dancer's, in respect of this, that it should stand ready and firm to meet onsets that are sudden and unexpected.

62. Constantly observe who those are whose approbation you wish to have, and what ruling principles they possess. For then you will neither blame those who offend involuntarily, nor will you want their approbation if you look to the sources of their opinions and appetites.

63. Every soul, the philosopher says, is involuntarily deprived of truth; consequently in the same way it is deprived of justice and temperance and benevolence and everything of the kind. It is most necessary to bear this constantly in mind, for thus you will be more gentle toward all.

64. In every pain let this thought be present, that there is no dishonor in it, nor does it make the governing intelligence worse, for it does not damage the intelligence either so far as the intelligence is rational or so far as it is social. Indeed in the case of most pains let this remark of Epicurus aid you, that pain is neither intolerable nor everlasting if you bear in mind that it has its limits, and if you add nothing to it in imagination: and remember this, too, that we do not perceive that many things that are disagreeable to us are the same as pain, such as excessive drowsiness, and being scorched by heat, and having no appetite. When then you are discontented about any of these things, say to yourself that you are yielding to pain.

65. Take care not to feel toward the inhuman as they feel toward men.

66. How do we know if Telauges was not superior in character to Socrates? For it is not enough that Socrates died a more noble death and disputed more skillfully with the sophists, and passed the night in the cold with more endurance, and that when he was bid to arrest Leon of Salamis, he considered it more noble to refuse, and that he walked in a swaggering way in the streets—though as to this fact one may have great doubts if it was true. But we ought to inquire, what kind of a soul it was that Socrates possessed, and if he was able to be content with being just toward men and pious toward the gods, neither idly vexed on account of men's villainy, nor yet making himself a slave to any man's ignorance, nor receiving as strange anything that fell to his share out of the universal, nor enduring it as intolerable, nor allowing his understanding to sympathize with the affects of the miserable flesh.

67. Nature has not so mingled the intelligence with the composition of the body as not to have allowed you the power of circumscribing yourself and of bringing under subjection to yourself all that is your own; for it is very possible to be a divine man and to be recognized as such by no one. Always bear this in mind; and another thing, too, that very little indeed is necessary for living a happy life. And because you have despaired of becoming a dialectician and skilled in the knowledge of nature, do not for this reason renounce the hope of being both free and modest and social and obedient to God.

68. It is in your power to live free from all compulsion in the greatest tranquillity of mind, even if all the world cry out against you as much as they choose, and even if wild beasts tear in pieces the members of this kneaded matter that has grown around you. For what hinders the mind in the midst of all this from maintaining itself in tranquillity and in a just judgment of all surrounding things and in a ready use of the objects that are presented to it? The judgment should be able to say to the thing that falls under its observation: This you are in substance (reality), though in men's opinion you may appear to be of a different kind; and the user shall say to that which falls under the hand: You are the thing that I was seeking; for to me that which presents itself is always a material for the exercise of both rational and political virtue, and in a word, for the exercise of art, which belongs to man or God. For everything that happens has a relationship either to God or man and is neither new nor difficult to handle, but is usual and apt matter to work on.

69. The perfection of moral character consists in this, in passing every day as if it were the last, and in being neither violently excited nor torpid nor playing the hypocrite.

70. The gods, who are immortal, are not vexed because during so long a time they must tolerate continually men such as they are, and so many of them bad: notwithstanding this, the gods also take care of them in all ways. But you, who are destined to end so soon, are you wearied of enduring the bad, and this, too, when you are one of them?

71. It is a ridiculous thing for a man not to fly from his own badness, which is indeed possible, but to fly from other men's badness, which is impossible.

72. Whatever the rational and political (social) faculty finds to be neither intelligent nor social, it properly judges to be inferior to itself.

73. When you have done a good act and another has received it, why do you look for a third thing besides these, as fools do, either to have the reputation of having done a good act or to obtain a return?

74. No man is tired of receiving what is useful. But it is useful to act according to nature. Do not then be tired of receiving what is useful by doing what is useful for others.

75. The nature of the All moved to make the universe. But now either everything that takes place comes by way of consequence or continuity; or even the chief things toward which the ruling power of the universe directs its own movement are governed by no rational principle. If this is remembered it will make you more tranquil in many things.

BOOK VIII

This reflection also tends to the removal of the desire for empty fame: that it is no longer in your power to have lived the whole of your life, or at the least your life from your youth upward, like a philosopher; but both to many others and to yourself it is plain that you are far from philosophy. You have fallen into disorder then, so that it is no longer easy for you to get the reputation of a philosopher; and your plan of life also opposes it. If then you have truly seen where the matter lies, throw away the thought of how you might seem to others, and be content if you live the rest of your life in the manner that your nature wills. Observe then what it wills, and let nothing else distract you; for you have had experience of many wanderings without having found happiness anywhere, not in syllogisms, nor in wealth, nor in reputation, nor in enjoyment, nor anywhere. Where is it then? It is in doing what man's nature requires. How then shall a man do this? If he has principles that are the source of his affects and his acts. What principles? Those that relate to good and bad: the belief that there is nothing good for man that does not make him just, temperate, manly, free; and that there is nothing bad that does not do the contrary to what has been mentioned.

2. On the occasion of every act ask yourself, How is this with respect to me? Will I regret it? A little time and I am dead, and all is gone. What more do I seek, if what I am now doing is the work of an intelligent living being, and a social being, and one who is under the same law with God?

3. Alexander and Gaius and Pompeius, what are they in comparison with Diogenes and Heraclitus and Socrates? For the latter were acquainted with things, and their causes (forms), and their matter, and the ruling principles of these men were the same. But as to the former, how many things had they to care for, and to how many things were they slaves.

4. Consider that men will do the same things even though you would burst with rage.

57

5. This is the chief thing: Do not be perturbed, for all things are according to the nature of the universal; and in a little time you will be nobody and nowhere, like Hadrian and Augustus. In the next place, having fixed your eyes steadily on your business, look at it, at the same time remembering that it is your duty to be a good man, and do what man's nature demands without turning aside; and speak as it seems to you most just, only let it be with a good disposition and with modesty and without hypocrisy.

6. The nature of the universal has this work to do, to remove to that place the things that are in this, to change them, to take them away hence, and to carry them there. All things are change, yet we need not fear anything new. All things are familiar to us; but the distribution of them still remains the same.

7. Every nature is contented with itself when it goes on its way well; and a rational nature goes on its way well when in its thoughts it assents to nothing false or uncertain, and when it directs its movements to social acts only, and when it confines its desires and aversions to the things that are in its power, and when it is satisfied with everything that is assigned to it by the common nature. For of this common nature every particular nature is a part, as the nature of the leaf is a part of the nature of the plant; except that in the plant the nature of the leaf is part of a nature that has not perception or reason, and is subject to being impeded; but the nature of man is part of a nature that is not subject to impediments, and is intelligent and just, since it gives to everything in equal portions and according to its worth, times, substance, cause (form), activity, and incident. But examine, not to discover that any one thing compared with any other single thing is equal in all respects, but by taking all the parts together of one thing and comparing them with all the parts together of another.

8. You have not leisure or ability to read. But you have leisure or ability to check arrogance: you have leisure to be superior to pleasure and pain: you have leisure to be superior to love of fame, and not to be vexed at stupid and ungrateful people, nay even to care for them.

9. Let no man any longer hear you finding fault with the court life or with your own.

10. Repentance is a kind of self-reproof for having neglected something useful; but that which is good must be something useful, and the perfect good man should look after it. But no such man would ever repent of having refused any sensual pleasure. Pleasure then is neither good nor useful.

11. This thing, what is it in itself, in its own constitution? What is its

substance and material? And what is causal nature (or form)? And what is it doing in the world? And how long does it subsist?

12. When you rise from sleep with reluctance, remember that it is according to your constitution and according to human nature to perform social acts, but sleeping is common also to irrational animals. But that which is according to each individual's nature is also more peculiarly its own, and more suitable to its nature, and indeed also more agreeable.

13. Constantly and, if it be possible, on the occasion of every impression on the soul, apply to it the principles of physics, ethics, and dialectics.

14. Whatever man you meet with, immediately say to yourself: What opinions has this man about good and bad? For if with respect to pleasure and pain and the causes of each, and with respect to fame and ignominy, death and life, he has such and such opinions, it will seem nothing wonderful or strange to me, if he does such and such things; and I shall bear in mind that he is compelled to do so.

15. Remember that as it is a shame to be surprised if the fig tree produces figs, so it is to be surprised if the world produces such and such things of which it is productive; and for the physician and the helmsman it is a shame to be surprised, if a man has a fever, or if the wind is unfavorable.

16. Remember that to change your opinion and to follow him who corrects your error is as consistent with freedom as it is to persist in your error. For it is your own activity, which is exerted according to your own movement and judgment, and indeed according to your own understanding, too.

17. If a thing is in your own power, why do you do it? But if it is in the power of another, whom do you blame? The atoms (chance) or the gods? Both are foolish. You must blame nobody. For if you can, correct that which is the cause; but if you cannot do this, correct at least the thing itself; but if you cannot do even this, of what use is it to you to find fault? For nothing should be done without a purpose.

18. That which has died does not fall out of the universe. If it stays here, it also changes here and is dissolved into its proper parts, which are elements of the universe and of yourself. And these, too, change, and they do not complain.

19. Everything exists for some end, be it a horse, a vine. Why do you wonder? Even the sun will say, I am for some purpose, and the rest of the gods will say the same. For what purpose then do you exist? To enjoy pleasure? See if common sense allows this.

20. Nature has included in its aim in every case no less the end than the beginning and the continuance, just like the man who throws up a ball. What good is it then for the ball to be thrown up, or harm for it to come down, or even to have fallen? And what good is it to the bubble while it holds together, or what harm when it is burst? The same way may be said of a light also.

21. Turn it (the body) inside out, and see what kind of thing it is; and when it has grown old, what kind of thing it becomes, and when it is diseased.

Short-lived are both the praiser and the praised, and the remember-er and the remembered: and all this in a nook of this part of the world; and not even here do all agree, no, not any one with himself: and the whole earth, too, is a point.

22. Attend to the matter before you, whether it is an opinion or an act or a word.

You suffer this justly: for you choose rather to become good tomorrow than to be good today.

23. Am I doing anything? I do it with reference to the good of mankind. Does anything happen to me? I receive it and refer it to the gods, and the source of all things, from which all that happens is derived.

24. As bathing appears to you—oil, sweat, dirt, filthy water, all things disgusting—so is every part of life and everything.

25. Lucilla saw Verus die, and then Lucilla died. Secunda saw Maximus die, and then Secunda died. Epitynchanus saw Diotimus die, and then Epitynchanus died. Antoninus saw Faustina die, and then Antoninus died. Such is everything. Celer saw Hadrian die, and then Celer died. And those sharp-witted men, either seers or men inflated with pride, where are they? For instance, the sharp-witted men, Charax and Demetrius the Platonist and Eudaimon, and anyone else like them. All ephemeral, dead long ago. Some indeed have not been remembered even for a short time, and others have become the heroes of fables, and again others have disappeared even from fables. Remember this then, that this little compound, yourself, must either be dissolved, or your poor breath must be extinguished, or be removed and placed elsewhere.

26. It brings satisfaction to a man to do the proper works of a man. Now it is a proper work of a man to be benevolent to his own kind, to despise the movements of the senses, to form a just judgment of plausible appearances, and to take a survey of the nature of the universe and of the things that happen in it.

27. There are three relations between you and other things: the one

to the body that surrounds you; the second to the divine cause from which all things come to all; and the third to those who live with you.

28. Pain is either an evil to the body—then let the body say what it thinks of it—or to the soul; but it is in the power of the soul to maintain its own serenity and tranquillity, and not to think that pain is an evil. For every judgment and movement and desire and aversion is within, and no evil ascends so high.

29. Wipe out your imaginings by often saying to yourself, "Now it is in my power to let no badness be in this soul, nor desire nor any perturbation at all; but looking at all things, I see their true nature, and I use each according to its value." Remember this power that nature gives you.

30. Speak both in the senate and to every man, whoever he may be, appropriately, without affectation: use plain discourse.

31. Augustus's court, wife, daughter, descendants, ancestors, sister, Agrippa, kinsmen, intimates, friends, Areius, Maecenas, physicians and sacrificing priests—the whole court is dead. Then turn to the rest, not considering the death of a single man, but of a whole race, as of the Pompeii; and that which is inscribed on the tombs, "The last of his race." Then consider what trouble those before them have had that they might leave a successor; and then, that of necessity some one must be the last. Again here consider the death of a whole race.

32. It is your duty to order your life well in every single act; and if every act does its duty, as far as is possible, be content; and no one is able to hinder you so that each act shall not do its duty. But something external will stand in the way. Nothing will stand in the way of your acting justly and soberly and considerately. "But perhaps some other active power will be hindered." Well, but by acquiescing in the hindrance and by being content to transfer your efforts to that which is allowed, another opportunity of action is immediately put before you in place of that which was hindered, and one which will adapt itself to this ordering of which we are speaking.

33. Receive wealth or prosperity without arrogance; and be ready to let it go.

34. If you have ever seen a hand cut off, or a foot, or a head, lying anywhere apart from the rest of the body, so does a man make himself, as far as he can, who is not content with what happens, and separates himself from others, or does anything unsocial. Suppose that you have detached yourself from the natural unity—for you were made by nature a part, but now you have cut yourself off—yet here there is this beautiful provision, that it is in your power to unite yourself again. God

has allowed this to no other part, after it has been separated and cut asunder, to come together again. But consider the kindness by which he has distinguished man, for he has put it in his power not to be separated at all from the universal; and when he has been separated, he has allowed him to return and to be united and to resume his place as a part.

35. As the nature of the universal has given to every rational being all the other powers that it has, so we have received from it this power also. For as the universal nature converts and fixes in its predestined place everything that stands in the way and opposes it, and makes such things a part of itself, so also the rational animal is able to make every hindrance its own material, and to use it for such purposes as it may have designed.

36. Do not disturb yourself by thinking of the whole of your life. Do not let your thoughts at once embrace all the various troubles that you may expect to befall you: but on every occasion ask yourself, What is there in this that is intolerable and past bearing? For you will be ashamed to confess. In the next place remember that neither the future nor the past pains you, but only the present. But this is reduced to a very little, if you only circumscribe it and chide your mind, if it is unable to hold out against even this.

37. Does Panthea or Pergamus now sit by the tomb of Verus? Does Chaurias or Diotimus sit by the tomb of Hadrian? That would be ridiculous. Well, suppose they did sit there, would the dead be conscious of it? And if the dead were conscious, would they be pleased? And if they were pleased, would that make them immortal? Was it not in the order of destiny that these persons, too, should first become old women and old men and then die? What then would those do after these were dead? All this is foul smell and blood in a bag.

38. If you can see sharp, look and judge wisely, says the philosopher.

39. In the constitution of the rational animal, I see no virtue that is opposed to justice; but I see a virtue that is opposed to love of pleasure, and that is temperance.

40. If you take away your opinion about that which appears to give you pain, you yourself stand in perfect security. "Who is this self?" Reason. "But I am not reason." Be it so. Let then reason not trouble itself. But if any other part of you suffers, let it have its own opinion about itself.

41. Hindrance to the perceptions of sense is an evil to the animal nature. Hindrance to the movements (desires) is equally an evil to the animal nature. And something else also is equally an impediment and

an evil to the constitution of plants. So then that which is a hindrance to the intelligence is an evil to the intelligent nature. Apply all these things then to yourself. Does pain or sensuous pleasure affect you? The senses will look to that. Has any obstacle opposed you in your efforts toward an object? If indeed you were making this effort absolutely (unconditionally, or without any reservation), certainly this obstacle is an evil to you considered as a rational animal. But if you take into consideration the usual course of things, you have not yet been injured or even impeded. Indeed, no one can impede the things that are proper to the mind. Neither fire, nor iron, nor tyrant, nor abuse, touches it in any way. "A sphere once formed remains round and true."

42. It is not fit that I should give myself pain, for I have never intentionally given pain even to another.

43. Different things delight different people. But it is my delight to keep the ruling faculty sound without turning away either from any man or from any of the things that happen to men, but looking at and receiving all with welcoming eyes and using everything according to its value.

44. See that you secure this present time to yourself: for those who rather pursue posthumous fame do not consider that the men of tomorrow will be exactly like these whom they cannot bear now; and both are mortal. And what is it in any way to you if these men of tomorrow utter this or that sound, or have this or that opinion about you?

45. Take me and cast me where you will; for there I shall keep my divine part tranquil, that is, content, if it can feel and act conformably to its proper constitution. Is this change of place sufficient reason why my soul should be unhappy and worse than it was, depressed, expanded, shrinking, affrighted? And what will you find that is sufficient reason for this?

46. Nothing can befall a man that is not a contingency natural to men; nor befall an ox, that is not natural to oxen, nor a vine, that is not natural to a vine, nor to a stone that is not proper to it. If then there happens to each thing both what is usual and natural, why should you complain? For the common nature brings nothing that you cannot bear.

47. If you are pained by any external thing, it is not this thing that disturbs you, but your own judgment about it. And it is in your power to wipe out this judgment now. But if anything in your own disposition gives you pain, who hinders you from correcting your opinion? And even if you are pained because you are not doing some particular thing that seems to you to be right, why do you not rather act than complain?

"But some insuperable obstacle is in the way." Do not be grieved then, for the cause of its not being done depends not on you. "But it is not worthwhile to live if this cannot be done." Take your departure then from life contentedly, just as he dies who is in full activity, and well pleased, too, with the things that are obstacles.

48. Remember that the ruling faculty is invincible, when, self-collected, it is satisfied with itself, if it does nothing that it does not choose to do, even if it resists from mere obstinacy. What then will it be when it forms a judgment about anything aided by reason and deliberately? Therefore the mind that is free from passions is a citadel, for man has nothing more secure to which he can fly for refuge and repel every attack. He then who has not seen this is an ignorant man; but he who has seen it and does not fly to this refuge is unhappy.

49. Say nothing more to yourself than what the first appearances report. Suppose that it has been reported to you that a certain person speaks ill of you. This has been reported; but that you have been injured, that has not been reported. I see that my child is ill. I do see; but that he is in danger, I do not see. Thus then always abide by the first appearances, and add nothing yourself from within, and then nothing happens to you. Or rather add something, but like a man who is familiar with every possible contingency in the world.

50. "A cucumber is bitter." Throw it away. "There are briars in the road." Turn aside from them. This is enough. Do not add, "And why were such things made in the world?" For you will be ridiculed by a man who is acquainted with nature, as you would be ridiculed by a carpenter and shoemaker if you found fault because you saw in their workshop shavings and cuttings from the things that they make. And yet they have places into which they can throw these shavings and cuttings, and the universal nature has no external space; but the wondrous part of her art is that though she has circumscribed herself, everything within her that appears to decay and to grow old and to be useless she changes into herself, and again makes other new things from these very same, so that she requires neither substance from without nor wants a place into which she may cast that which decays. She is content then with her own space, and her own matter and her own art.

51. Neither in your actions be sluggish nor in conversation without method, nor wandering in your thoughts, nor let there be in your soul inward contention nor external effusion, nor in life be so busy as to have no leisure.

Suppose that men kill you, cut you in pieces, curse you. What then can these things do to prevent your mind from remaining pure, wise, sober, just? For instance, if a man should stand by a limpid pure spring and curse it, the spring never ceases sending up potable water; and if he should cast clay into it or filth, it will speedily disperse them and wash them out, and will not be at all polluted. How then shall you possess a perpetual fountain and not a mere well? By forming yourself hourly to freedom conjoined with contentment, simplicity, and modesty.

52. He who does not know what the world is does not know where he is. And he who does not know for what purpose the world exists, does not know who he is, or what the world is. But he who has failed in any one of these things could not even say for what purpose he exists himself. What then do you think of him who avoids or seeks the praise of those who applaud, of men who know not either where they are or who they are?

53. Do you wish to be praised by a man who curses himself three times every hour? Would you wish to please a man who does not please himself? Does a man please himself who repents of nearly everything that he does?

54. No longer let your breathing only act in concert with the air that surrounds you, but let your intelligence also now be in harmony with the intelligence that embraces all things. For the intelligent power is diffused in all parts and pervades all things for him who is willing to draw it to him no less than the aerial power for him who can breathe.

55. Generally, wickedness does no harm at all to the universe; and particularly, the wickedness of one man does no harm to another. It is harmful only to him who has it in his power to be released from it as soon as he shall choose.

56. To my own free will the free will of my neighbor is just as indifferent as his poor breath and flesh. For though we are made especially for the sake of one another, still the ruling power of each of us has its own office, for otherwise my neighbor's wickedness would be my harm; and this was not God's will, in order that my unhappiness may not depend on another.

57. The sun appears to be poured down, and in all directions indeed it is diffused, yet it does not effuse itself away. For this diffusion is extension: Accordingly its rays are called extensions ($\alpha\kappa\tau\iota\nu\epsilon\sigma$) because they are extended ($\alpha\pi o\ \tau o\upsilon\ \epsilon\kappa\tau\epsilon\iota\nu\epsilon o\theta\alpha\iota$). But one may judge what kind of a thing a ray is if he looks at the sun's light passing through a narrow opening into a darkened room, for it is extended in a straight line, and is divided when it meets with any solid body that stands in the way and intercepts the air beyond; but there the light remains fixed and does not

glide or fall off. Such then ought to be the outpouring and diffusion of the understanding, never a diffusing away but an extension, and it should make no violent or impetuous collision with the obstacles that are in its way; nor yet fall down, but be fixed and enlighten that which received it. For a body will deprive itself of the illumination if it does not admit it.

58. He who fears death fears either the loss of sensation or a different kind of sensation. But if you shall have no sensation, neither will you feel any harm; and if you will acquire another kind of sensation, you will be a different kind of living being and you will not cease to live.

59. Men exist for the sake of one another. Teach them then or bear with them.

60. In one way an arrow moves, in another way the mind. Yet the mind, both when it cautiously examines its ground and when it is engaged in its inquiry, is nonetheless moving straight ahead and toward its goal.

61. Enter into every man's ruling faculty; and also let every other man enter into yours.

BOOK IX

Injustice is impiety. For since the universal nature has made rational animals for the sake of one another to help one another according to their deserts, but in no way to injure one another, he who transgresses her will is clearly guilty of impiety toward the highest divinity. And he, too, who lies is guilty of impiety to the same divinity; for the universal nature is the nature of things that are; and things that are have a relation to all things that come into existence. And further, this universal nature is named truth and is the prime cause of all things that are true. He then who lies intentionally is guilty of impiety inasmuch as he acts unjustly by deceiving; and he also who lies unintentionally, inasmuch as he is at variance with the universal nature, and inasmuch as he disturbs the order by fighting against the nature of the world; for he fights against it who is moved of himself to that which is contrary to truth. And whereas he had previously been endowed by nature with the means of distinguishing false from true, by neglecting to use them, he has lost the power. And indeed he who pursues pleasure as good and avoids pain as evil is guilty of impiety. For of necessity such a man must often find fault with the universal nature, alleging that it assigns things to the bad and the good contrary to their deserts, because frequently the bad are in the enjoyment of pleasure and possess the things that procure pleasure, but the good have pain for their share and the things that cause pain. And further, he who is afraid of pain will sometimes also be afraid of some of the things that will happen in the world, and even this is impiety. And he who pursues pleasure will not abstain from injustice, and this is plainly impiety.

But those who are of one mind with nature and would walk in her ways must hold a neutral attitude toward those things toward which the universal nature is neutral—for she would not be the maker of both were she not neutral toward both. With respect to pain, then, and pleasure, or death and life, or honor and dishonor, which the universal nature treats with neutrality, whoever is not equally neutral is manifestly acting impiously. And by the universal nature treating these with

67

neutrality I mean that all things happen neutrally in a chain of sequence to things that come into being and to their afterproducts by some primeval impulse of Providence, in accordance with which she was impelled by some primal impulse to this making of an ordered universe, when she had conceived certain principles for all that was to be, and allocated the powers generative of beings and changes and successions such as we see.

2. It would be a man's happiest lot to depart from mankind without having had any taste of lying and hypocrisy and luxury and pride. However, to breathe out one's life when a man has had enough of these things is the next best voyage, as the saying goes. Or have you determined to abide with vice, and has experience not yet induced you to fly from this pestilence? For the destruction of the understanding is a pestilence, much more indeed than any such corruption and change of this atmosphere that surrounds us. For the latter corruption is a pestilence of animals so far as they are animals; but the former is a pestilence of men so far as they are men.

3. Do not despise death, but be well content with it, since this, too, is one of those things that nature wills. For such as it is to be young and to grow old, and to increase and to reach maturity, and to have teeth and beard and grey hairs, and to beget, and to be pregnant and to bring forth, and all the other natural operations that the seasons of your life bring, such also is dissolution. This, then, is consistent with the character of a reflecting man, to be neither careless nor impatient nor contemptuous with respect to death, but to wait for it as one of the operations of nature. As you now wait for the time when the child shall come out of your wife's womb, so be ready for the time when your soul shall fall out of this envelope. But if you require also a vulgar kind of comfort that shall reach your heart, you will be made best reconciled to death by observing the objects from which you are going to be removed, and the morals of those with whom your soul will no longer be mingled. For it is no way right to be offended with men, but it is your duty to care for them and to bear with them gently; and yet to remember that your departure will be not from men who have the same principles as yourself. For this is the only thing, if there be any, that could draw us the contrary way and attach us to life, to be permitted to live with those who have the same principles as ourselves. But now you see how great is the trouble arising from the discord of those who live together, so that you may say, "Come quick, O death, lest perchance I, too, should forget myself."

4. He who does wrong does wrong against himself. He who acts unjustly acts unjustly to himself, because he makes himself bad.

5. He often acts unjustly who does not do a certain thing; not only he who does a certain thing.

6. Your present opinion founded on understanding, and your present conduct directed to social good, and your present disposition of contentment with everything that happens—that is enough.

7. Wipe out imagination: check desire: extinguish appetite: keep the ruling faculty in its own power.

8. Among irrational animals one life is distributed, and among reasonable animals one intelligent soul is distributed: just as there is one earth of all things that are of an earthly nature, and we see by one light, and breathe one air, all of us that have the faculty of vision and all that have life.

9. All that share in a common element have an affinity for their own kind. Everything that is earthy turns toward the earth, everything that is liquid flows together, and everything that is of an aerial kind does the same, so that they require something to keep them asunder, and the application of force. Fire indeed moves upward on account of the elemental fire, but it is so ready to be kindled together with all the fire that is here, that even every substance that is somewhat dry is easily ignited, because there is less mingled with it of that which is a hindrance to ignition. Accordingly then everything also that participates in the common intelligent nature moves in like manner toward that which is of the same kind with itself, or moves even more. For so much as it is superior in comparison with all other things, in the same degree also is it more ready to mingle with and to be fused with that which is akin to it.

Accordingly among animals devoid of reason we find swarms of bees, and herds of cattle, and the nurture of young birds, and in a manner, erotic passion; for even in animals there are souls, and the power that brings them together is seen to exert itself in the superior degree, and in such a way as never has been observed in plants or in stone or in trees. But in rational animals there are political communities and friendships, and families and meetings of people; and in wars, there are treaties and armistices. But in the things that are still superior, even though they are separated from one another, unity in a manner exists, as in the stars. Thus the ascent to the higher degree is able to produce a sympathy even in things that are separated.

See, then, what now takes place. For only intelligent animals have now forgotten this mutual desire and inclination, and in them alone the property of flowing together is not seen. But still though men strive to avoid this union, they are caught and held by it, for their nature is too strong for them; and you will see what I say, if you only observe. It is easier, at any rate, to find an earthy thing in touch with nothing earthy than a man wholly severed from mankind.

10. Man and God and the universe all produce fruit, each at the proper season. It does not matter that in common parlance these terms are associated with the vine and like things. Reason produces fruit both for all and for itself, and there are produced from it other things of the same kind as reason itself.

11. If you are able, correct by teaching those who do wrong; but if you cannot, remember that indulgence is given to you for this purpose. And the gods, too, are indulgent to such persons; and for some purposes they even help them to get health, wealth, reputation; so kind are they. And it is in your power also; or say, who hinders you?

12. Labor not as one who is wretched, nor yet as one who would be pitied or admired: but direct your will to one thing only: to act or not to act as social reason requires.

13. Today I have got out of all trouble, or rather I have cast out all trouble, for it was not outside, but within and in my opinions.

14. All things are the same, familiar in experience, and ephemeral in time, and worthless in matter. Everything now is just as it was in the time of those whom we have buried.

15. Things stand outside of us, themselves by themselves, neither knowing anything of themselves nor expressing any judgment. What is it, then, that passes judgment on them? The ruling faculty.

16. Not in passivity, but in activity lie the evil and the good of the rational social animal, just as his virtue and his vice lie not in passivity, but in activity.

17. For the stone that has been thrown up it is no evil to come down, nor indeed any good to have been carried up.

18. Penetrate inward into men's leading principles, and you will see what judges you are afraid of, and what kind of judges they are of themselves.

19. All things are changing: and you yourself are in continuous mutation and in a manner in continuous destruction, and the whole universe, too.

20. It is your duty to leave another man's wrongful act there where it is.

21. Termination of activity, cessation from movement and opinion, and, in a sense, their death, is no evil. Turn your thoughts now to the consideration of your life, your life as a child, as a youth, your man-

hood, your old age, for in these also every change was a death. Is this anything to fear? Turn your thoughts now to your life under your grandfather, then to your life under your mother, then to your life under your father; and as you find many other differences and changes and terminations, ask yourself, "Is this anything to fear?" In like manner, then, neither are the termination and cessation and change of your whole life a thing to be afraid of.

22. Hasten to examine your own ruling faculty and that of the universe and that of your neighbor: your own that you may make it just: and that of the universe, that you may remember of what you are a part; and that of your neighbor, that you may know whether he has acted ignorantly or with knowledge, and that you may also consider that his ruling faculty is akin to yours.

23. As you yourself are a component part of a social system, so let every act of yours be a component part of social life. Whatever act of yours then has no reference either immediately or remotely to a social end, this tears asunder your life and does not allow it to be one, and it is of the nature of a mutiny, just as when in a popular assembly a man acting by himself stands apart from the general agreement.

24. Children's squabbles and make-believe, and "little souls bearing up corpses"—the invocation of the dead might strike one as a more vivid reality!

25. Examine that which makes a thing what it is, its formative cause, and, isolating it from the material, contemplate it; then determine the longest time that a thing of this peculiar form is naturally made to endure.

26. You have endured infinite troubles through not being contented with your ruling faculty's doing the things that it is constituted by nature to do. But enough of this.

27. When another blames you or hates you, or when men say anything injurious about you, approach their poor souls, penetrate within, and see what kind of men they are. You will discover that there is no reason to be concerned that these men have this or that opinion about you. You must, however, be well disposed toward them, for by nature they are friends. And the gods, too, aid them in all ways, by dreams, by signs, toward the attainment of those things on which they set a value.

28. The periodic movements of the universe are the same, up and down from age to age. And either the universal intelligence puts itself in motion for every separate effect, and if this is so, be content with that which results from its activity; or it puts itself in motion once, and everything else comes by way of sequence in a manner; or indivisible

elements are the origin of all things. In a word, if there is a god, all is well; and if chance rules, do not also be governed by it.

Soon the earth will cover us all: then the earth, too, will change, and the things also that result from change will continue to change forever, and these again forever. For if a man reflects on the changes and transformations that follow one another like wave after wave and their rapidity, he will despise everything that is perishable.

29. The universal cause is like a winter torrent: it carries everything along with it. But how worthless are all these poor people who are engaged in matters political, and, as they suppose, are playing the philosopher! All drivellers. Well then, man: do what nature now requires. Set yourself in motion, if it is in your power, and do not look about you to see if anyone will observe it; nor yet expect Plato's *Republic*: but be content if the smallest thing goes on well, and consider such an event to be no small matter. For who can change men's opinions? And without a change of opinions what else is there than the slavery of men who groan while they pretend to obey? Come now and tell me of Alexander and Philip and Demetrius of Phalerum. They themselves shall judge whether they discovered what the common nature required, and trained themselves accordingly. But if they acted like tragic heroes, no one has condemned me to imitate them. The work of philosophy is simple and modest. Do not draw me aside into pomposity.

30. Look down from above on the countless herds of men and their countless solemnities, and the infinitely varied voyagings in storms and calms, and the varieties of those who are born, who live together, and die. And consider, too, the life lived by others long ago, and the life of those who will live after you, and the life now lived among barbarous nations, and how many have never even heard your name, and how many will soon forget it, and how they who perhaps now are praising you will very soon blame you, and that neither a posthumous name is of any value, nor reputation, nor anything else.

31. Let there be freedom from perturbations with respect to the things that come from the external cause; and let there be justice in the things done by virtue of the internal cause, that is, let there be movement and action terminating in this, in social acts, for this is according to your nature.

32. You can rid yourself of many useless things among those that disturb you, for they lie entirely in your imagination; and you will then gain for yourself ample space by comprehending the whole universe in your mind, and by contemplating the eternity of time, and observing

the rapid change of every part of everything, how short is the time from birth to dissolution, and the illimitable time before birth as well as the equally boundless time after dissolution.

33. All that you see will quickly perish, and those who have been spectators of its dissolution will very soon perish, too. And he who dies at the extremest old age will be brought into the same condition with him who died prematurely.

34. What are these men's leading principles, and about what kind of things are they busy, and for what kind of reasons do they love and honor? Imagine that you see their poor souls laid bare. When they think that they do harm by their blame or good by their praise, what an idea!

35. Loss is nothing else than change. But the universal nature delights in change, and in obedience to her all things are now done well, and from eternity have been done in like form, and will be such to time without end. What, then, do you say? That all things have been and all things always will be bad, and that no power has ever been found in so many gods to rectify these things, but the world has been condemned to be bound in never-ceasing evil?

36. The rottenness of the matter that is the foundation of everything! Water, dust, bones, filth; or again, marble rocks are mere callosities of the earth; and gold and silver, the sediments; and garments, only bits of hair; and purple dye, blood; and everything else is of the same kind. And that which is of the nature of breath is also another thing of the same kind, changing from this to that.

37. Enough of this wretched way of life and grumbling and apish tricks. Why are you disturbed? What is there new in this? What unsettles you? Is it the form of the thing? Look at it. Or is it the matter? Look at it. But besides these there is nothing. Toward the gods, then, now become at last simpler and better. It is the same whether we examine these things for a hundred years or three.

38. If any man has done wrong, the harm is his own. But perhaps he has not done wrong.

39. Either all things proceed from one intelligent source and come together as in one body, and the part ought not to find fault with what is done for the benefit of the whole; or there are only atoms, and nothing else than mixture and dispersion. Why, then, are you disturbed? Say to the ruling faculty, "Are you dead, corrupted, are you playing the hypocrite, have you become a beast, do you herd and feed with the rest?"

40. Either the gods have no power or they have power. If, then, they have no power, why do you pray to them? But if they have power, why

do you not pray for them to give you the faculty of not fearing any of the things that you fear, or of not desiring any of the things that you desire, or not being pained at anything, rather than pray that they should grant this or refuse that? For certainly if they can cooperate with men, they can cooperate for these purposes. But perhaps you will say, the gods have placed this in your power. Well, then, is it not better to use what is in your power like a free man than to desire in a slavish and ·abject way what is not in your power? And who has told you that the gods do not aid us even in the things that are in our power? Begin, then, to pray for such things, and you will see. One man prays thus: How might I sleep with that woman? Do you pray: How shall I not desire to sleep with her? Another prays thus: How shall I be released from this? Another prays: How shall I not desire to be released? Another thus: How shall I not be afraid to lose him? In fine, turn your prayers this way, and see what comes.

41. Epicurus says, "In my sickness my conversation was not about my bodily sufferings, nor did I talk about such subjects to those who visited me; but I continued to discourse on the nature of things as before, keeping to this main point, how the mind, while participating in such movements as go on in the poor flesh, shall be free from perturbations and maintain its proper good. Nor did I," he says, "give the physicians an opportunity of putting on solemn looks, as if they were doing something great, but my life went on well and happily." Do, then, the same that he did both in sickness, if you are sick, and in any other circumstances; never desert philosophy in any events that may befall you, nor hold trifling talk either with an ignorant man or with one unacquainted with nature—this is a principle of all schools of philosophy; remain intent only on that which you are now doing and on the instrument by which you do it.

42. When you are offended with any man's shameless conduct, immediately ask yourself, Is it possible, then, that shameless men should not be in the world? It is not possible. Do not, then, require what is impossible. For this man also is one of those shameless men who must of necessity be in the world. Let the same considerations be present to your mind in the case of the knave and the faithless man, and of every man who does wrong in any way. For at the same time that you remind yourself that it is impossible that such men should not exist, you will become more kindly disposed toward everyone individually. It is also useful to perceive, as soon as the occasion arises, what virtue nature has given to man to oppose to every wrongful act. For as

an antidote against the stupid man, she has given mildness, and against another kind of man some other power.

And in all cases it is possible for you to correct by teaching the man who has gone astray; for every man who errs misses his object and has gone astray. Besides, wherein have you been injured? For you will find that no one among those against whom you are irritated has done anything by which your mind could be made worse; but that which is evil to you and harmful has its foundation only in the mind.

Where is the harm or the strangeness in the boor acting like a boor? See whether you are not yourself the more to blame in not expecting that he would err in such a way. For you had means given you by your reason to suppose that it was likely that he would commit this error, and yet you have forgotten and are amazed that he has erred.

But most of all, when you blame a man as faithless or ungrateful, turn to yourself. For the fault is manifestly your own, whether you trusted that a man who had such a disposition would keep his promise, or when conferring your kindness you did not confer it absolutely, nor yet in such way as to have received full recompense simply from having done it. For what more do you want when you have done a man a service? Are you not content that you have done something conformable to your nature? Do you seek to be paid for it? It is as if the eye were to demand a recompense for seeing, or the feet for walking. For as these members are formed for a particular purpose, and by working according to their separate constitutions obtain what is their own, so also as man is formed by nature to acts of benevolence; when he has done anything benevolent or in any other way conducive to the common interest, he has acted conformably to his constitution, and he gets what is his own.

BOOK X

Will you, then, my soul, never be good and simple and one and naked, more manifest than the body that surrounds you? Will you never enjoy an affectionate and contented disposition? Will you never be full and without a want of any kind, longing for nothing more, nor desiring anything, either animate or inanimate, for the enjoyment of pleasures? Nor yet desiring time wherein you shall have longer enjoyment, or place, or pleasant climate, or society of men with whom you might live in harmony? But will you be satisfied with your present condition, and pleased with all that is around you, and will you convince yourself that you have everything and that it comes from the gods, that everything is well for you, and will be well whatever shall please them, and whatever they shall give for the conservation of the perfect living being, the good and just and beautiful, which generates and holds together all things, and contains and embraces all things that are dissolved for the production of other like things? Will you never be such that you shall so dwell in community with gods and men as neither to find fault with them at all, nor to be condemned by them?

2. Observe what your nature requires, so far as you are governed by nature only: then do it and accept it, if your nature, so far as you are a living being, shall not be made worse by it. And next you must observe what your nature requires so far as you are a living being. And all this you may allow yourself, if your nature, so far as you are a rational animal, shall not be made worse by it. But the rational animal is consequently also a political (social) animal. Use these rules, then, and trouble yourself about nothing else.

3. Everything that happens either happens in such way as you are formed by nature to bear it, or as you are not formed by nature to bear it. If, then, it happens to you in such way as you are formed by nature to bear it, do not complain, but bear it accordingly. But if it happens in such way as you are not formed by nature to bear it, do not complain, for it will perish after it has consumed you. Remember, however, that you are formed by nature to bear everything whose tolerability depends

76

on your own opinion to make it so, by thinking that it is in your interest or duty to do so.

4. If a man is mistaken, instruct him kindly and show him his error. But if you are not able, blame yourself, or not even yourself.

5. Whatever may happen to you, it was prepared for you from all eternity; and the implication of causes was from eternity spinning the thread of your being and that which is incident to it.

6. Whether the universe is a concourse of atoms, or nature is a system, let this first be established: that I am a part of the whole that is governed by nature; next, that I stand in some intimate connection with other kindred parts. For remembering this, inasmuch as I am a part, I shall be discontented with none of the things that are assigned to me out of the whole; for nothing is injurious to the part if it is for the advantage of the whole. For the whole contains nothing that is not for its advantage; and all natures indeed have this common principle, but the nature of the universe has this principle besides, that it cannot be compelled even by any external cause to generate anything harmful to itself. By remembering, then, that I am a part of such a whole, I shall be content with everything that happens. And inasmuch as I am in a manner intimately related to kindred parts, I shall do nothing unsocial, but I shall rather direct myself to the things that are akin to me, and I shall turn all my effort to the common interest and withhold it from the contrary. Now, if these things are done so, life must flow on happily, just as you may observe that a happy citizen is one who continues a course of action that is advantageous to his fellow-citizens and is content with whatever the state may assign to him.

7. The parts of the whole, everything, I mean, that is naturally comprehended in the universe, must of necessity perish (*perish* in the sense of "undergo change"). But if this is naturally both an evil and a necessity for the parts, the whole would not continue to exist in good condition, the parts being subject to change and constituted so as to perish in various ways. Did nature herself design to do evil to the things that are parts of herself, and to make them subject to evil and of necessity fall into evil, or have such results happened without her knowing it? Both of these suppositions, indeed, are incredible.

But if a man should even drop the term nature (as an efficient power), and should speak of these things as natural, even then it would be ridiculous to affirm at the same time that the parts of the whole are in their nature subject to change and at the same time to be surprised or vexed as if something were happening contrary to nature, particularly as the dissolution of things is into those things of which each thing is composed. For there is either a dispersion of the elements out of which everything has been compounded, or a change from the solid to the earthy and from the airy to the aerial, so that these parts are taken back into the universal reason, whether this at certain periods is consumed by fire or renewed by eternal changes. And do not imagine that the solid and the airy part belong to you from the time of generation. For all this received its accretion only yesterday and the day before, as one may say, from the food eaten and the air breathed. What changes, then, is that which has received the accretion, not that which your mother brought forth. But suppose that this which your mother brought forth implicates you very much with that other part, which has the peculiar quality of change: this has no bearing on the present argument.

8. When you have assumed these names—good, modest, truthful, rational, a man of equanimity, and magnanimous—take care that you do not change these names; and if you should lose them, quickly return to them. And remember that the term "rational" was intended to signify a discriminating attention to every object and freedom from negligence; and that "equanimity" is the voluntary acceptance of the things that are assigned to you by the common nature; and that "magnanimity" is the elevation of the intelligent part above the pleasurable or painful sensations of the flesh, and above that poor thing called fame, and death, and all such things. If, then, you maintain yourself in the possession of these names, without desiring to hear them addressed to you by others, you will be another person and will enter on another life. For to continue to be such as you have hitherto been, and to be torn in pieces and defiled in such a life, is the character of a very stupid man and one overfond of his life, like those half-devoured fighters with wild beasts who, though covered with wounds and gore, still beg to be kept to the following day, though they will be exposed in the same state to the same claws and bites.

Therefore fix yourself in the possession of these few names: and if you are able to abide in them, abide as if you were removed to certain Isles of the Blessed. But if you feel yourself adrift and cannot maintain your hold, go courageously into some nook where you can maintain them, or even depart at once from life, not in passion, but with simplicity and freedom and modesty, after doing this one laudable thing at least in your life, to have gone out of it thus. In order, however, to hold to the remembrance of these names, it will greatly help you if you remember the gods, and that they wish not to be flattered, but wish all reasonable beings to be made like themselves; and remember that what does the work of a fig tree is a fig tree, and that what does the work of a dog is a dog, and that what does the work of a bee is a bee, and that what does the work of a man is a man.

9. Play-acting, war, astonishment, torpor, slavery, will daily wipe out those holy principles of yours. How many things without studying nature do you imagine, and how many do you neglect? But it is your duty to look on and to do everything in such a way that simultaneously you carry through the present task, give full play to the faculty of pure thought, and achieve the confidence that comes from maintaining a knowledge, unobtruded yet unconcealed, of each individual thing. For when will you enjoy simplicity, when gravity, and when the knowledge of each individual thing, both what it is in substance, and what place it has in the universe, and how long it is formed to exist and of what things it is compounded, and to whom it can belong, and who are able both to give it and take it away?

10. A spider is proud when it has caught a fly; one man when he has caught a poor hare, and another when he has taken a little fish in a net, and another when he has taken wild boars, and another when he has taken bears, and another when he has taken Sarmatians. Are not these robbers, if you examine their opinions?

11. Acquire the contemplative way of seeing how all things change into one another, and constantly attend to it, and exercise yourself about this part of philosophy. For nothing is so much adapted to produce magnanimity. Such a man has put off the body, and as he sees that he must, no one knows how soon, go away from among men and leave everything here, he gives himself up entirely to just doing in all his actions, and in everything else that happens, he resigns himself to the universal nature. But as to what any man shall say or think about him or do against him, he never even thinks of it, being himself contented with these two things, with acting justly in what he now does, and being satisfied with what is now assigned to him; and he lays aside all distracting and busy pursuits, and desires nothing else than to accomplish the straight course through the law, and by accomplishing the straight course to follow God.

12. What need is there of suspicious fear, since it is in your power to inquire what ought to be done? And if you see clearly, go by this way content, without turning back: but if you do not see clearly, stop and take the best advisers. But if any other things oppose you, go on according to your powers with due consideration, keeping to that which appears to be just. For it is best to reach this object, and if you fail, let your failure be in attempting this. He who follows reason in all things

is both tranquil and active at the same time, and also cheerful and collected.

13. Inquire of yourself as soon as you wake from sleep, whether it will make any difference to you if another does what is just and right. It will make no difference.

You have not forgotten, I suppose, that those who assume arrogant airs in bestowing their praise or blame on others are such as they are in bed and at board, and you have not forgotten what they do, and what they avoid and what they pursue, and how they steal and how they rob, not with hands and feet, but with their most valuable part, by means of which there is produced, when a man chooses, fidelity, modesty, truth, law, a good daimon (happiness)?

14. To her who gives and takes back all, to nature, the man who is instructed and modest says, "Give what you will; take back what you will." And he says this not proudly, but obediently and well pleased with her.

15. You have but a short time left to live. Live as on a mountain. For it makes no difference whether a man lives there or here, if he lives everywhere in the world as in a state (political community). Let men see, let them know a real man who lives according to nature. If they cannot endure him, let them kill him. For that is better than to live thus as men do.

16. No longer talk at all about the kind of man that a good man ought to be, but be such.

17. Constantly contemplate the whole of time and the whole of substance, and consider that all individual things as to substance are a seed of a fig, and as to time, the turning of a gimlet.

18. Look at everything that exists, and observe that it is already in dissolution and in change, and as it were putrefaction or dispersion, or that everything is so constituted by nature as to die.

19. Consider what men are when they are eating, sleeping, coupling, evacuating, and so forth. Then what kind of men they are when they are imperious and arrogant, or angry and scolding from their elevated place. But a short time ago to how many they were slaves and for what things; and after a little time consider in what a condition they will be.

20. What the universal nature brings to everything is for the benefit of that thing. And it is for its benefit at the time when nature brings it.

21. "The earth is in love with showers, and the majestic sky is in love." And the universe loves to make whatever is about to be. I say then to the universe that I love as you love. And is not this too said, that "this

or that loves to happen"?

22. Either you live here and have already accustomed yourself to it, or you are going away, and this was your will; or you are dying and have discharged your duty. But besides these things there is nothing. Be of good cheer, then.

23. Let this always be plain to you, that this piece of land is like any other; and that all things here are the same as things on the top of a mountain, or on the seashore, or wherever you choose to be. For you will find just what Plato says, "Dwelling within the walls of a city as in a shepherd's fold on a mountain," and milking flocks.

24. What is my ruling faculty now to me? And of what nature am I now making it? And for what purpose am I now using it? Is it void of understanding? Is it loosed and rent asunder from social life? Is it melted into and mixed with the poor flesh so as to move together with it?

25. He who flies from his master is a runaway; but the law is master, and he who breaks the law is a runaway. And he also who is grieved or angry or afraid, is dissatisfied because something has been or is or shall be of the things that are appointed by him who rules all things, and he is law, and assigns to every man what is fit. He then who fears or is grieved or is angry is a runaway.

26. A man deposits seed in a womb and goes away, and then another cause takes it and labors on it and makes a child. What a thing from such a material! Again, the child passes food down through the throat, and then another cause takes it and makes perception and motion, and in fine life and strength and other things; how many and how strange! Observe then the things that are produced in such a hidden way, and see the power just as we see the power that carries things downward and upward—not with the eyes, but still no less plainly.

27. Constantly consider how all things such as they now are, in time past also were; and consider that they will be the same again. And place before your eyes entire dramas and stages of the same form, whatever you have learned from your experience or from older history; for example, the whole court of Hadrian, and the whole court of Antoninus, and the whole court of Philip, Alexander, Croesus; for all those were dramas such as we see now, only with different actors.

28. Imagine every man who is grieved at anything or discontented to be like a pig that is sacrificed and kicks and screams.

Like this pig also is he who on his bed in silence laments the bonds in which we are held. And consider that only to the rational animal is it given to follow voluntarily what happens; but simply to follow is a necessity imposed on all.

29. In everything that you do, pause and ask yourself if death is a dreadful thing because it deprives you of this.

30. When you are offended at any man's fault, immediately turn to yourself and reflect in what manner you yourself have erred: for example, in thinking that money is a good thing or pleasure, or a bit of reputation, and the like. For by attending to this you will quickly forget your anger if you consider that the man is compelled: for what else could he do? Or, if you are able, take away from him the compulsion.

31. When you have seen Satyron the Socratic, think of either Eutyches or Hymen, and when you have seen Euphrates, think of Eutychion or Silvanus, and when you have seen Alciphron, think of Tropaeophorus, and when you have seen Xenophon, think of Crito or Severus, and when you have looked at yourself, think of one of the Caesars, and so by analogy in every case. Then let this thought be in your mind: Where are they now? Nowhere, or nobody knows where. For thus continuously you will look at human things as smoke and as nothing at all; especially if you reflect at the same time that what has once changed will never exist again throughout eternity. But you, in what a brief space of time is your existence? And why are you not content to pass through this short time in an orderly way? What matter and opportunity for your activity are you avoiding? For what else are all these things, except exercises for the reason, when it has viewed carefully and by examination into their nature the things that happen in life? Persevere then until you have made these things your own, as a strong stomach assimilates every food, as the blazing fire makes flame and brightness out of everything that is thrown into it.

32. Let it not be in any man's power to say truly of you that you are not simple or that you are not good; if anyone thinks anything of this kind about you, let him be a liar; and this is altogether in your power. For who is he that will hinder you from being good and simple? Resolve then to live no longer unless you shall be such. For neither does reason allow you to live, if you are not such.

33. Taking our material into account, what can be done or said in the way most conformable to reason? For whatever this may be, it is in your power to do it or to say it, and do not make excuses that you are hindered. You will not cease to lament until you find that the utilizing, in a manner consistent with the constitution of man, of the material presented to you and cast in your way shall be to you what indulgence is to the sensual; for a man ought to consider as an enjoyment everything which it is in his power to do according to his own nature. And it is in his power everywhere. Now, it is not given to a cylinder to move

everywhere by its own motion, nor yet to water nor to fire, nor to anything else that is governed by nature or an irrational soul, for the things
that check them and stand in the way are many. But intelligence and
reason are able to go through everything that opposes them, and in
such manner as they are formed by nature and as they choose. Place
before your eyes this facility with which reason will be carried through
all things, as fire upward, as a stone downward, as a cylinder down an
inclined surface, and seek for nothing further. For all other obstacles
either affect the body only, which is a dead thing, or, except through
opinion and the yielding of the reason itself, they do not crush or do
any harm of any kind; for if they did, he who felt it would immediately become bad.

Now, in the case of all things that have a certain constitution, whatever harm may happen to any of them, that which is so affected
becomes consequently worse; but in such a case, a man becomes both
better, if one may say so, and more worthy of praise by making a right
use of these accidents. And finally remember that nothing harms him
who is really a citizen, which does not harm the state; nor yet does anything harm the state, which does not harm law (order); and of the
things that are called misfortunes, not one harms law. What then does
not harm law does not harm either state or citizen.

34. To him who is penetrated by true principles, any common precept, even the briefest, is sufficient to remind him that he should be
free from grief and fear. For example:

> Leaves: some the wind scatters on the ground—
> So is the race of men.

Leaves, also, are your children; and leaves, too, are they who cry out as
if they were worthy of credit and bestow their praise, or on the contrary
curse, or secretly blame and sneer; and leaves, in like manner, are those
who shall receive and transmit a man's fame to later times. For all such
things as these "are produced in the season of spring," as the poet says;
then the wind casts them down; then the forest produces other leaves
in their places. But a brief existence is common to all things, and yet
you avoid and pursue all things as if they would be eternal. A little time,
and you will close your eyes; and whoever has attended you to your
grave soon will lament another.

35. The healthy eye ought to see all visible things and not say, "I wish
for green things"; for this is the condition of a diseased eye. And the
healthy hearing and smelling ought to be ready to perceive all that can
be heard and smelled. And the healthy stomach ought to be with
respect to all food just as the mill with respect to all things that it is

formed to grind. And accordingly the healthy understanding ought to be prepared for everything that happens; but that which says, "Let my dear children be safe, and let all men praise whatever I may do," is an eye that seeks for green things or teeth that seek for soft things.

36. There is no man so fortunate that there shall not be by him when he is dying some who are pleased with what is going to happen. Suppose that he was a good and wise man, will there not be at last someone to say to himself, "Let us at last breathe freely being relieved from this schoolmaster? It is true that he was harsh to none of us, but I perceived that he tacitly condemned us." This is what is said of a good man. But in our own case how many other things are there for which there are many who wish to get rid of us. You will consider this then when you are dying, and you will depart more contentedly by reflecting thus: I am going away from a life in which even my associates, in behalf of whom I have striven so much, prayed, and cared, themselves wish me to depart, hoping perchance to get some little advantage by it. Why then should a man cling to a longer stay here? Do not, however, for this reason go away less kindly disposed to them, but preserving your own character, friendly and benevolent and mild, and not as if you were torn away; but rather should your withdrawal from them be as that gentle slipping away of soul from body that we can see when a man makes a peaceful end. For nature united you to them, and now she dissolves the union. I am separated as from kinsmen—not, however, dragged while resisting, but without compulsion; for this, too, is one of the things according to nature.

37. Accustom yourself as much as possible, on the occasion of anything being done by any person, to inquire with yourself, For what object is this man doing this? But begin with yourself, and examine yourself first.

38. Remember that this which pulls the strings is the thing that is hidden within: this is the power of persuasion, this is life, this, if one may say so, is man. In contemplating yourself, never include the vessel that surrounds you and these organs that are attached to it. For they are like an axe, differing only in this that they grow from the body. For indeed, without the cause that moves and checks them, there is no more use in these parts than in the weaver's shuttle, the writer's pen, and the driver's whip.

BOOK XI

These are the properties of the rational soul: it sees itself, analyzes itself, makes itself such as it chooses, itself reaps its own fruits—whereas the fruits of the vegetable kingdom and the corresponding produce of animals are reaped by others. The soul obtains its own end, wherever the limit of life may be fixed. Not as in a dance and in a play and in such things, where the whole action is incomplete if anything cuts it short; but in every part and wherever it may be stopped, it makes what has been set before it full and complete, so that it can say, "I have what is my own." And further it traverses the whole universe and the surrounding void, and surveys its form, and it extends itself into the infinity of time, and embraces and comprehends the periodic renovation of all things, and it comprehends that those who come after us will see nothing new, nor have those before us seen anything more, but in a manner he who is forty years old, if he has any understanding at all, has seen, by virtue of the uniformity that prevails, all things that have been and all that will be. This, too, is a property of the rational soul, love of one's neighbor, and truth and modesty, and to value nothing more than itself, which is also the property of law. Thus then right reason differs not at all from the reason of justice.

2. You will set little value on pleasant song and dancing and the pancratium,* if you will analyze the melody of the voice into its several sounds, and ask yourself as to each, "Am I mastered by this?"; for you will be ashamed to confess it. The same holds for dancing, if at each movement and posture you will do a similar analysis; and the like also in the matter of the pancratium. In all things, then, except virtue and the acts of virtue, remember to apply yourself to their several parts, and by this division to come to value them little: and apply this rule also to your whole life.

3. What a great soul is that which is ready, at any requisite moment, to be separated from the body and then to be extinguished or dispersed

---

*An ancient Greek athletic competition combining wrestling and boxing.

85

or continue to exist. But this readiness must come from a man's own judgment, not from mere obstinacy, as with the Christians, but considerately and with dignity and in a way to persuade another, without tragic show.

4. Have I done something for the general interest? Well then I have had my reward. Let this always be present to your mind, and never stop doing such good.

5. What is your art? To be good. And how is this accomplished well except by general principles, some about the nature of the universe, and others about the proper constitution of man?

6. At first tragedies were brought on the stage as means of reminding men of the things that happen to them, and that it is according to nature for things to happen so, and that, if you are delighted with what is shown on the stage, you should not be troubled with what takes place on the larger stage. For you see that these things must be gone through, and that even they bear them who cry out "O Cithaeron." And, indeed, some things are said well by the dramatic writers, especially the following:

> Me and my children if the gods neglect,
> This has its reasons, too.

And again:

> We must not chafe and fret at that which happens.

And:

> Reap life's harvest like the wheat's fruitful ear.

And other things of the same kind.

After tragedy the old comedy was introduced, which had a magisterial freedom of speech, and by its very plainness of speaking was useful in reminding men to beware of insolence; and for this purpose, too, Diogenes used to take from these writers.

But as to the middle comedy, which came next, observe what it was, and again, for what object the new comedy was introduced, which gradually sank down into a mere mimic artifice. That some good things are said even by these writers, everybody knows: but the whole plan of such poetry and dramaturgy, to what end does it look!

7. How plain does it appear that there is not another condition of life so well suited for philosophizing as this in which you now happen to be.

8. A branch cut off from the adjacent branch must of necessity be cut off from the whole tree also. So, too, a man, when he is separated from

another man, has fallen off from the whole social community. Now as to a branch, another cuts it off, but a man by his own act separates himself from this neighbor when he hates him and turns away from him, and he does not know that he has at the same time cut himself off from the whole social system. Yet he has this privilege certainly from Zeus, who framed society, for it is in our power to grow again to that which is near to us, and again to become a part that helps to make up the whole. However, if this kind of separation happens often, it makes it difficult for the seceding part to be brought to unity and to be restored to its former condition. Finally, the branch that from the first grew together with the tree and has continued to have one life with it, is not like that which has been cut off and then grafted onto it. For this is something like what the gardeners mean when they say it grows with the rest of the tree but that it is not of one mind with it.

9. As those who try to stand in your way when you are proceeding according to right reason will not be able to turn you aside from your proper action, so neither let them drive you from your benevolent feelings toward them, but be on your guard equally in both matters, not only in the matter of steady judgment and action, but also in the matter of gentleness toward those who try to hinder or otherwise trouble you. For this also is a weakness, to be vexed at them, as well as to be diverted from your course of action and to give way through fear; for both are equally deserters from their post, the man who does it through fear, and the man who is alienated from him who is by nature a kinsman and a friend.

10. There is no nature that is inferior to art, for the arts imitate the nature of things. But if this is so, that nature which is the most perfect and the most comprehensive of all natures cannot fall short of the skill of art. Now all arts do the inferior things for the sake of the superior; therefore the universal nature does so, too. And, indeed, hence is the origin of justice, and in justice the other virtues have their foundation: for justice will not be observed, if we either care for indifferent things or are easily deceived and careless and changeable.

11. If the things do not come to you, the pursuit and avoidance of which disturb you, still in a manner you are seeking them out. Let then your judgment about them be at rest, and they will remain quiet, and you will not be seen either pursuing or avoiding.

12. The spherical form of the soul maintains its figure when it is neither extended toward any object nor contracted inward, neither dispersed nor sinking down, but is illuminated by light, by which it sees the truth, the truth of all things and the truth that is in itself.

13. Suppose any man shall despise me. Let him look to that himself. But I will look to this, that I be not discovered doing or saying anything deserving of contempt. Shall any man hate me? That will be his affair. But I will be mild and benevolent toward every man, and ready to show even him his mistake, not reproachfully, nor yet as making a display of my endurance, but nobly and honestly, like the great Phocion, unless indeed he only assumed it. For the interior parts ought to be such, and a man ought to be seen by the gods neither dissatisfied with anything nor complaining. For what evil is it to you if you are now doing what is agreeable to your own nature, and are satisfied with that which at this moment is suitable to the nature of the universe, since you are a human being placed at your post in order that what is for the common advantage may be done in some way?

14. Men despise one another and flatter one another; and men wish to raise themselves above one another, and crouch before one another.

15. How unsound and insincere is he who says, "I have determined to deal with you in a fair way." What are you doing, man? There is no occasion to give this notice. It will soon show itself by acts. The voice ought to be plainly written on the forehead. Such as a man's character is, he immediately shows it in his eyes, just as he who is beloved forthwith reads everything in the eyes of lovers. The man who is honest and good ought to be exactly like a man who smells strong, so that the bystander, as soon as he comes near him, must smell the odor whether he chooses to or not. But the affectation of simplicity is like a crooked stick. Nothing is more disgraceful than a wolfish friendship (false friendship). Avoid this most of all. The good and simple and benevolent show all these things in the eyes, and there is no mistaking it.

16. As to living in the best way, this power is in the soul, if it be indifferent to things that are indifferent. And it will be indifferent, if it looks on each of these things separately and all together, and if it remembers that not one of them produces in us an opinion about itself, nor comes to us; but these things remain immovable, and it is we ourselves who produce the judgments about them, and, as we may say, write them in ourselves, it being in our power not to write them, and it being in our power, if perchance these judgments have imperceptibly got admission to our minds, to wipe them out; and if we remember also that such attention will only be for a short time, and then life will be at an end. Besides, what trouble is there at all in doing this? For if these things are according to nature, rejoice in them, and they will be easy to you: but if contrary to nature, seek what is conformable to your own nature, and

strive toward this, even if it brings no reputation; for every man is allowed to seek his own good.

17. Consider whence each thing has come, of what it consists, and into what it changes, and what kind of a thing it will be when it has changed, and that it will sustain no harm.

18. If any have offended you, consider first: What is my relation to men, and that we are made for one another; and in another respect, I was made to be set over them, as a ram over the flock or a bull over the herd. But examine from first principles, from this: If all things are not mere atoms, it is nature that orders all things: if this is so, the inferior things exist for the sake of the superior, and these for the sake of one another.

Second, consider what kind of men they are at the table, in bed, and so forth: and particularly, under what compulsions of opinion they operate; and as to their acts, consider with what pride they do what they do.

Third, that if men do rightly what they do, we ought not to be displeased; but if they do not right, it is plain that they do so involuntarily and in ignorance. For as every soul is unwillingly deprived of the truth, so also is it unwillingly deprived of the power of behaving to each man according to his deserts. Accordingly men are pained when they are called unjust, ungrateful, and greedy, and, in a word, wrongdoers to their neighbors.

Fourth, consider that you also do many things wrong, and that you are a man like others; and even if you do abstain from certain faults, still you have the disposition to commit them, though either through cowardice, or concern about reputation, or some such mean motive, you abstain from such faults.

Fifth, consider that you do not even understand whether men are doing wrong or not, for many things are done with a certain reference to circumstances. And in short, a man must learn a great deal to enable him to pass a correct judgment on another man's acts.

Sixth, consider when you are much vexed or grieved, that man's life is only a moment, and after a short time we are all laid out dead.

Seventh, that it is not men's acts that disturb us, for those acts have their foundation in men's ruling principles, but it is our own opinions that disturb us. Take away these opinions then, and resolve to dismiss your judgment about an act as if it were something grievous, and your anger is gone. How then shall I take away these opinions? By reflecting that no wrongful act of another brings shame on you: for unless that which is shameful is alone bad, you also must of necessity do many things wrong, and become a robber and everything else.

Eighth, consider how much more pain is brought on us by the anger and vexation caused by such acts than by the acts themselves at which we are angry and vexed.

Ninth, consider that a good disposition is invincible, if it is genuine and not an affected smile and acting a part. For what will the most violent man do to you if you continue to be of a kind disposition toward him, and if, as opportunity offers, you gently admonish him and calmly correct his errors at the very time when he is trying to do you harm, saying, "Not so, my child, we are constituted by nature for something else. I shall certainly not be injured, but you are injuring yourself, my child." And show him with gentle tact and by general principles that this is so, and that even bees do not do as he does, nor any animals that are formed by nature to be gregarious. But you must do this not in irony or by way of rebuke, but with kindly affection and without any bitterness at heart, not as from a master's chair, nor yet to impress the bystanders, but as if he were indeed alone even though others are present.

Remember these nine rules, as if you had received them as a gift from the Muses, and begin at last to be a man while you live. But you must equally avoid flattering men and being vexed at them, for both are unsocial and lead to harm. And let this truth be present to you in the excitement of anger, that to be moved by passion is not manly, but that mildness and gentleness, as they are more agreeable to human nature, so also are they more manly; and he who possesses these qualities possesses strength, nerves, and courage, and not the man who is subject to fits of passion and discontent. For in the degree to which a man's mind is nearer to freedom from all passion, in the same degree also is it nearer to strength: and as the sense of pain is a characteristic of weakness, so also is anger. For he who yields to pain and he who yields to anger are both wounded and both submit.

But if you will, receive also a tenth present from the leader of the Muses (Apollo), and it is this—that to expect bad men not to do wrong is madness, for he who expects this desires an impossibility. But to allow men to behave so to others, and to expect them not to do you any wrong, is irrational and tyrannical.

19. There are four principal aberrations of the superior faculty against which you should be constantly on your guard, and when you have detected them, you should wipe them out and say on each occasion thus: this thought is not necessary; this tends to destroy social union; this which you are going to say comes not from the real thoughts—for you should consider it among the most absurd of things for a man not to speak from his real thoughts. But the fourth is when

you shall reproach yourself for anything, for this is an evidence of the diviner part within you being overpowered and yielding to the less honorable and to the perishable part, the body, and to its gross pleasures.

20. Thy aerial part and all the fiery parts that are mingled in you, though by nature they have an upward tendency, still in obedience to the disposition of the universe they are overpowered here in the compound mass (the body). And also the whole of the earthy part in you and the watery, though their tendency is downward, still are raised up and occupy a position that is not their natural one. In this manner then the elemental parts obey the universal, for when they have been fixed in any place perforce they remain there until again the universal shall sound the signal for dissolution. Is it not then strange that only your intelligent part should be disobedient and discontented with its own place? And yet no force is imposed on it, but only those things that are conformable to its nature: still it does not submit, but is carried in the opposite direction. For the movement toward injustice and intemperance and to anger and grief and fear is nothing else than the act of one who deviates from nature. And also when the ruling faculty is discontented with anything that happens, then, too, it deserts its post: for it is constituted for piety and reverence toward the gods no less than for justice. For these qualities also are comprehended under the generic term of contentment with the constitution of things, and indeed they are prior to acts of justice.

21. He who has not one and always the same object in life cannot be one and the same all through his life. But what I have said is not enough, unless this also is added: what this object ought to be. For as there is not the same opinion about all the things that in some way or other are considered by the majority to be good, but only about some certain things, that is, things that concern the common interest; so also ought we to propose to ourselves an object that shall be of a common kind (social) and political. For he who directs all his own efforts to this object, will make all his acts alike, and thus will always be the same.

22. Think of the country mouse and of the town mouse, and of the alarm and trepidation of the town mouse.

23. Socrates used to call the opinions of the many by the name of Lamiae [ghouls], bugbears to frighten children.

24. The Lakedaimonians at their public spectacles used to set seats in the shade for strangers, but they themselves sat down anywhere.

25. Socrates excused himself to Perdiccas for not going to him, saying, "It is because I would not perish by the worst of all ends," that is, I would not receive a favor and then be unable to return it.

26. In the writings of the Ephesians there was this precept: constantly to think of one of the men of former times who practiced virtue.

27. The Pythagoreans bid us in the morning look to the heavens that we may be reminded of those bodies that continually do the same things and in the same manner perform their work, and also be reminded of their purity and nudity. For there is no veil over a star.

28. Consider what a man Socrates was when he dressed himself in a skin, after Xanthippe had taken his cloak and gone out, and what Socrates said to his friends who were ashamed of him and drew back from him when they saw him dressed thus.

29. Neither in writing nor in reading will you be able to lay down rules for others before you shall have first learned to obey rules yourself. Much more is this so in life.

30. "You are a slave: free speech is not for you."

31. "And my heart laughed within."

32. "And virtue they will curse, speaking harsh words."

33. "To look for the fig in winter is a madman's act: such is he who looks for his child when he may no longer have one."

34. "When a man kisses his child," said Epictetus, "he should whisper to himself, 'To-morrow perchance you will die.'" But those are words of bad omen. "No word is a word of bad omen," said Epictetus, "that expresses any work of nature; or if it is so, it is also a word of bad omen to speak of the ears of corn being reaped."

35. The unripe grape, the ripe bunch, the dried grape, all are changes, not into nothing, but into something that exists not yet.

36. According to Epictetus, "No man can rob us of our free will."

37. Epictetus also said, "A man must discover an art (or rules) with respect to giving his assent; and in respect to his movements he must be careful that they be made with regard to circumstances, that they be consistent with social interests, that they have regard to the value of the object; and as to sensual desire, he should altogether keep away from it; and as to avoidance (aversion) he should not show it with respect to any of the things that are not in our power."

38. "The dispute then," he said, "is not about any common matter, but about being mad or not."

39. Socrates used to say, "'What do you want? Souls of rational men or irrational?' 'Souls of rational men.' 'Of what rational men? Sound or unsound?' 'Sound.' 'Why then do you not seek for them?' 'Because we have them.' 'Why then do you fight and quarrel?'"

BOOK XII

All those things at which you wish to arrive by a circuitous road, you can have now, if you do not refuse them to yourself. That is to say, if you will take no notice of all the past, and trust the future to Providence, and direct the present in the way of piety and justice: piety, that you may be content with the lot that is assigned to you, for nature designed it for you and you for it; justice, that you may always speak the truth freely and without disguise, and do the things that are agreeable to law and according to the worth of each. And let neither another man's wickedness hinder you, nor opinion nor voice, nor yet the sensations of the poor flesh that has grown about you; for the passive part will look to this.

If then, whatever the time may be when you shall be near to your departure, neglecting everything else, you shall respect only your ruling faculty and the divinity within you, and if you shall be afraid not because you must some time cease to live, but if you shall fear never to have begun to live according to nature—then you will be a man worthy of the universe that has produced you, and you will cease to be a stranger in your native land, and to wonder at things that happen daily as if they were something unexpected, and to be dependent on this or that.

2. God sees the minds (ruling principles) of all men bared of the material vesture and rind and impurities. For with His intellectual part alone He touches the intelligence only, which has flowed and been derived from Himself into these bodies. And if you also use yourself to do this, you will rid yourself of much trouble. For he who has little regard for the poor flesh that envelops him surely will not trouble himself over clothing and dwelling and fame and other such externals and show.

3. You are composed of three things: body, breath (life), intelligence. Of these the first two are yours insofar as it is your duty to take care of them; but the third alone is truly yours. Therefore if you shall separate from yourself, that is, from your understanding, whatever others do or

93

say, and whatever you have done or said yourself, and whatever future things trouble you because they may happen, and whatever in the body that envelops you or in the breath (life), which is by nature associated with the body, is attached to you independent of your will, and whatever the external circumambient vortex whirls around you, so that the intellectual power, exempt from the things of fate, can live pure and free by itself, doing what is just and accepting what happens and saying the truth: if you will separate, I say, from this ruling faculty the things that are attached to it by the impressions of sense, and the things of time to come and of time that is past, and will make yourself like Empedocles' sphere, "All round, and in its joyous rest reposing," and if you shall strive to live what is really your life, that is, the present—then you will be able to pass that portion of life that remains for you up to the time of your death, free from perturbations, nobly, and obedient to your own daimon (to the god that is within you).

4. I have often wondered how it is that every man loves himself more than all the rest of men, but yet sets less value on his own opinion of himself than on the opinion of others. If then a god or a wise teacher should present himself to a man and bid him to think of nothing and to design nothing that he would not express as soon as he conceived it, he could not endure it even for a single day. So it is clear that we accord much more respect to what our neighbors think of us than to what we think of ourselves.

5. How can it be that the gods, after having arranged all things well and benevolently for mankind, have overlooked this alone, that some men and very good men, and men who, as we may say, have had most communion with the divinity, and through pious acts and religious observances have been most intimate with the divinity, should when once dead have no second existence but be wholly extinguished?

But if this is so, be assured that if it ought to have been otherwise, the gods would have done it. For if it were just, it would also be possible; and if it were according to nature, nature would have had it so. But because it is not so, if in fact it is not so, be assured that it ought not to have been so: for you can easily see that in this inquiry you are disputing with the deity; and we should not thus dispute with the gods unless they were most excellent and most just; but if this is so, they would not have allowed anything in the ordering of the universe to be neglected unjustly and irrationally.

6. Practice that also wherein you have no expectation of success. For even the left hand, which is ineffectual for all other things for want of practice, holds the bridle more vigorously than the right hand; for it has been practiced in this.

7. Consider in what condition both in body and soul a man should be when he is overtaken by death; and consider the shortness of life, the boundless abyss of time past and future, the feebleness of all matter.

8. Contemplate the formative principles (forms) of things bare of their coverings; the purposes of actions; consider what pain is, what pleasure is, and death, and fame. See who is to blame for a man's inner unrest; how no man is hindered by another; that everything is opinion.

9. In the application of your principles you must be like the pancratiast, not like the gladiator.* For the latter lays aside the blade he uses, and takes it up again, but the former always has his hand and needs only to clench it.

10. See what things are in themselves, dividing them into matter, form, and purpose.

11. What a power man has to do nothing except what God will approve, and to accept all that God may give him.

12. With respect to that which happens conformably to nature, we ought to blame neither gods, for they do nothing wrong either voluntarily or involuntarily, nor men, for they do nothing wrong except involuntarily. Consequently we should blame nobody.

13. How ridiculous and what a stranger he is who is surprised at anything that happens in life.

14. Either there is a fatal necessity and invincible order, or a kind Providence, or a confusion without a purpose and without a director. If then there is an invincible necessity, why do you resist? But if there is a Providence that allows itself to be propitiated, make yourself worthy of the help of the divinity. But if there is a confusion without a governor, be content that in such a tempest you have yourself a certain ruling intelligence. And even if the tempest carries you away, let it carry away the poor flesh, the poor breath, everything else; for the intelligence at least it will not carry away.

15. Does the light of the lamp shine without losing its splendor until it is extinguished; and shall the truth that is in you and justice and temperance be extinguished before your death?

16. When a man appears to have done something wrong, say, "How then do I know if this is a wrongful act?" And even if he has done wrong, how do I know that he has not condemned himself, in effect tearing his own face? Consider that he who would not have the bad man do wrong is like the man who would not have the fig tree secrete acrid juice in its fruit and would not have infants cry and the horse neigh, and whatever

---

*Or, *like the the prizefighter, not like the the duelist.*

else must of necessity be. For what must a man do who has such a character? If then you are irritable, cure this disposition.

17. If it is not right, do not do it: if it is not true, do not say it. For let your impulse be in your own power.

18. In everything always observe what the thing is that produces for you an appearance, and resolve it by dividing it into the formal, the material, the purpose, and the time within which it must end.

19. Perceive at last that you have in you something better and more divine than the things that cause the various affects, and as it were pull you by the strings. What is there now in my mind? Is it fear, or suspicion, or desire, or anything of the kind?

20. First, do nothing inconsiderately or without a purpose. Second, make your acts refer to nothing else but a social end.

21. Consider that before long you will be nobody and nowhere, nor will any of the things exist that you now see, nor any of those who are now living. For all things are formed by nature to change and be turned and to perish in order that other things in continuous succession may exist.

22. Consider that everything is opinion, and opinion is in your power. Take away then, when you choose, your opinion, and like a mariner who has rounded the headland, you will find calm, everything stable, and a waveless bay.

23. Any one activity, whatever it may be, when it has ceased at its proper time, suffers no evil because it has ceased; nor does he who has done this act suffer any evil because the act has ceased. In like manner then the whole that consists of all the acts, which is our life, suffers no evil if it has ceased at its proper time; nor does the agent suffer in that it has ceased to act. Similarly then if life, that sum total of all our acts, ceases in its own good time, it suffers no ill from this very fact, nor is he ill served who has brought this chain of acts to an end in its own due time. The due season and the terminus are fixed by universal nature (at times even by our individual nature, as with old age), the constant change of whose parts keeps the whole universe ever youthful and in its prime. All that is advantageous to the whole is ever fair and in its bloom. The ending of life then is not only no evil to the individual—for it brings him no disgrace, if in fact it is both outside our choice and not inimical to the general weal—but a good, since it is timely for the universe, bears its share in it, and is borne along with it. For then is he who is borne along on the same path as God, and borne in his judgment toward the same things, indeed a man god-borne.

24. You must have these three principles in readiness: First, do noth-

ing either inconsiderately or otherwise than as justice herself would act; and with respect to what may happen to you from without, consider that it happens either by chance or according to Providence, and you must neither blame chance nor accuse Providence. Second, consider what every being is from the seed to the time of its receiving a soul, and from the reception of a soul to the giving back of the same, and of what things every being is compounded and into what things it is resolved. Third, if you should suddenly be raised up above the earth, and should look down on human things and observe their infinite variety, you will despise them. If at that time you should also see at a glance how great is the number of beings who dwell all around in the air and the ether, consider that as often as you should be raised up, you would see the same things, sameness of form and shortness of duration. Are these things to be proud of?

25. Cast away opinion and you are saved. Who then hinders you from casting it away?

26. When you are troubled about anything, you have forgotten that all things happen according to the universal nature; and forgotten that a man's wrongful act is nothing to you; and further you have forgotten that everything that happens always happened so and will happen so, and now happens so everywhere; forgotten, too, how close is the kinship between a man and the whole human race, for it is a community, not of a little blood or seed, but of intelligence. And you have forgotten this, too, that every man's intelligence is a god, and is an emanation from the deity; and forgotten this, that nothing is a man's own, but that his child and his body and his very soul came from the deity; forgotten this, that everything is opinion; and lastly you have forgotten that every man lives the present time only, and loses only this.

27. Constantly recall those who have complained greatly about anything, those who have been most conspicuous by the greatest fame or misfortunes or enmities or fortunes of any kind: then think, Where are they all now? Smoke and ash and a tale, or not even a tale. Take any instance of this sort, how Fabius Catullinus lived in the country, and Lucius Lupus in his gardens, and Stertinius at Baiae, and Tiberius at Capreae and Velius Rufus (or Rufus at Velia); and in fine think of the eager pursuit of anything conjoined with pride; and how worthless everything is after which men violently strain; and how much more philosophical it is for a man in the opportunities presented to him to show himself just, temperate, obedient to the gods, and to do this with all simplicity: for the pride that is proud of its want of pride is the most intolerable of all.

28. To those who ask, "Where have you seen the gods or how do you comprehend that they exist and so worship them," I answer, in the first place, they may be seen even with the eyes;* in the second place neither have I seen even my own soul and yet I honor it. Thus then with respect to the gods, from what I constantly experience of their power, from this I comprehend that they exist and I venerate them.

29. The security of life is this, to examine everything all through, what it is itself, what is its material, what the formal part; with all your soul to do justice and to say the truth. What remains except to enjoy life by joining one good thing to another so as not to leave even the smallest intervals between?

30. There is one light of the sun, though it is interrupted by walls, mountains, and other things infinite. There is one common substance, though it is distributed among countless bodies that have their separate qualities. There is one soul, though it is distributed among infinite natures and individual circumscriptions (or individuals). There is one intelligent soul, though it seems to be divided. Now in the things that have been mentioned all the other parts, such as those that are air and matter, are without sensation and have no ties of affinity: and yet even these parts are knit together by the faculty of intelligence and the gravitation that draws them together. But intellect in a peculiar manner tends to that which is of the same kin, and combines with it, and the feeling of social fellowship is not interrupted.

31. What do you wish? To continue to exist? Well, do you wish to have sensation? Movement? Growth? And then again to cease to grow? To use your speech? To think? What is there of all these things that seems to you worth desiring? But if it is easy to set little value on all these things, turn to that which remains, which is to follow reason and God. But it is inconsistent with honoring reason and God to be troubled because by death a man will be deprived of the other things.

32. How small a part of the boundless and unfathomable time is assigned to every man! For it is very soon swallowed up in the eternal. And how small a part of the whole substance! And how small a part of the universal soul! And on what a small clod of the whole earth you creep! Reflecting on all this, consider nothing to be great except to act as your nature leads you, and to endure that which the common nature brings.

33. How does the ruling faculty make use of itself? For all lies in this.

---

*According to Haines, "The stars were gods in the Stoic view."

But everything else, whether it is in the power of your will or not, is only lifeless ashes and smoke.

34. This reflection is most adapted to move us to contempt of death: that even those who think pleasure to be a good and pain an evil still have despised it.

35. Not even death can bring terror to him who regards that alone as good which comes in due season, and to whom it is all one whether his acts in conformity to right reason are few or many, and a matter of indifference whether he look upon the world for a longer or a shorter time.

36. Man, you have been a citizen in this great state (the world): what difference does it make to you whether for five years or a hundred? For under its laws equal treatment is meted out to all. What hardship then is there in being banished from the city, not by a tyrant or an unjust judge but by nature, who brought you into it? So might a praetor who has employed an actor dismiss him from the stage. "But I have not played my five acts, but only three." Very possibly, but in life three acts are the whole drama; for what shall be a complete drama is determined by Him who was once the cause of its composition, and now of its dissolution: but you are the cause of neither. Depart then satisfied, for He also who releases you is satisfied.